STUDIES IN MAJOR LITERARY AUTHORS

Edited by

William E. Cain
Professor of English
Wellesley College

A ROUTLEDGE SERIES

Studies in Major Literary Authors

William E. Cain, *General Editor*

DOROTHY WORDSWORTH'S ECOLOGY

Kenneth R. Cervelli

Routledge
New York & London

Routledge
Taylor & Francis Group
270 Madison Avenue
New York, NY 10016

Routledge
Taylor & Francis Group
2 Park Square
Milton Park, Abingdon
Oxon OX14 4RN

© 2007 by Taylor & Francis Group, LLC
Routledge is an imprint of Taylor & Francis Group, an Informa business

Printed in the United States of America on acid-free paper
10 9 8 7 6 5 4 3 2 1

International Standard Book Number-10: 0-415-98037-2 (Hardcover)
International Standard Book Number-13: 978-0-415-98037-1 (Hardcover)

Library of Congress Cataloging-in-Publication Data

Cervelli, Kenneth R., 1964-
    Dorothy Wordsworth's ecology / by Kenneth R. Cervelli.
        p. cm. -- (Studies in major literary authors)
        Includes bibliographical references (p.   ) and index.
    ISBN 0-415-98037-2
    1. Wordsworth, Dorothy, 1771-1855--Criticism and interpretation. 2. Ecology in literature. 3. Romanticism--England. I. Title.

PR5849.C47 2007
828'.703--dc22   2006039062

Visit the Taylor & Francis Web site at
http://www.taylorandfrancis.com

and the Routledge Web site at
http://www.routledge.com

For LuAnne

Contents

Acknowledgments

I happily trace the origins of this project back to a graduate seminar on the Romantics I took with Dr. Scott McEathron while working on my doctorate at Southern Illinois University at Carbondale. One of the critical texts we examined was Jonathan Bate's *Romantic Ecology*, and while I didn't know at the time just how much Bate's work would influence me, the impact of Dr. McEathron's passionate teaching and thinking was immediate. He went on to direct my dissertation, giving me much needed advice and support while I worked back here in Canada. My heartfelt thanks, then, most definitely go to him. Dr. Ken K. Collins was the chief catalyst in my decision to specialize in nineteenth-century literature at SIU. He possesses an unmatchable elegance and poise in the classroom, and his seminar on the Victorian novel remains one of the highlights in my intellectual development. I thank him for—well, *everything*, but I would especially like to thank him for teaching me how to write a more polished sentence. Dr. Jane Cogie expertly guided me in the process of tutoring students, observed my teaching, and also served on my dissertation committee. She has always, however, been extraordinarily generous with her time. Dr. Lisa McClure's good humor helped new graduate students settle in during those first hot days in Carbondale, and I continue to benefit from her humane insights into pedagogy. I enjoyed many pleasant conversations with Dr. Anne Chandler (most frequently held in the hallways of Faner Hall), and I thank her for agreeing to be on my dissertation committee at the last minute.

Readers will immediately recognize the enormous debt I owe to the work of Susan Levin, Jonathan Bate, Karl Kroeber, and James McKusick. I might sometimes disagree with their arguments, but they have given me a great deal to ponder, and I continue to learn from them. Thanks also to Professor Levin for allowing me to quote liberally from her groundbreaking book, *Dorothy Wordsworth and Romanticism*.

Like other students of Dorothy Wordsworth, I remain in awe of the brilliant scholarship and editorial work of Pamela Woof. Her insights are interwoven throughout this study, and thanks to her I now feel as though I have actually been out walking with the Wordsworths.

I discovered the work of Gary Snyder back in the early nineties, and his life-affirming vision continues to shape my sense of humankind's place on this earth. I thank him for allowing me to quote from "For/From Lew," as well as for suggesting that I quote his arresting poem in its entirety.

My office mates at Mount Royal College (Erika Watters, Janet Bowes, and Jill Boettger) and the University of Calgary (Jason Wiens and Lynda Hall) helped me keep my sanity while I taught between the two schools and worked at my writing. Faculty and Staff at both schools have always been extraordinarily accommodating—I only wish I had more time to stick around and chat! And the many students I have taught over the years have been a constant source of inspiration. In particular, I would like to thank the members of English 519.28 ("Rooted Wanderers"): Jessie Bryant, Shelagh Burrowes, Fraser Calderwood, Karol Cheetham, Cindy Drover-Davidson, Jeff Jennens, Carmen Mathes, Anindita Mukherjee, Mariam Radhwi, Jason Salter, Adam Vuong, and Caleb Zimmerman.

Fellow Romanticist Tim Ziegenhagen not only gave me a copy of Jonathan Bate's *The Song of the Earth* at *just* the right moment (thus properly igniting this project), he has always willingly read and generously commented on my work. Our continued correspondence keeps the flame of friendship brightly lit. Paul and Deanna Odney were our neighbors for three wonderful years in Carbondale, but they were our friends before that time, and they remain our great friends today (along with new additions to the family, Owen and Keegan—the happy band encircling). I met Katie Harse and Lin Ho-You while working in Canterbury's Bookshop, and their good humor and friendship have sustained me through it all. In particular, I would like to thank Katie for the exquisite conversations at the Good Earth, as well as for kindly photocopying several key items for me. I thank Lin for helping me appreciate more fully the significance of E. M. Forster's work, as well as for supplying us with the many MST3K episodes. Palmer Olson continues to astound me with his incredible knowledge of all things book-related. And Dr. Janis Svilpis, who taught me while I was an undergraduate at the University of Calgary, remains an inspirational teaching model to this day.

My parents and I left California together and moved to Canada when I was sixteen years old, a move that ultimately led me to discover the joys of post-secondary education. I thank them from the bottom of my heart for their constant kindness and undying support. My sister, Lesley, stayed back in California, but she never feels far away. Without my knowing it at the time, my childhood friend, Robert Neely, taught me that "The Child is father of the Man," and I continue to learn from his wise ways. My wife's family helped us move back and forth (twice) between the United States and Canada so that we could pursue graduate work; they also continue to help us in smaller—and no less significant—ways.

I would not have been able to sustain the energy needed for this project without the music that means the most to me: jazz.

This book is dedicated to LuAnne, my companion for life. She introduced me to the wonders of literature and literary study back when we first met, and the gentle touch of her hand ensures the well-being of our happy, diversely populated ecosystem.

PERMISSIONS

"For/From Lew" from *Axe Handles* (San Francisco: North Point Press, 1983) by Gary Snyder, copyright by Gary Snyder, reprinted by permission of the author.

Excerpts *Dorothy Wordsworth and Romanticism* (New Brunswick: Rutgers, 1987) by Susan Levin, copyright by Susan Levin, reprinted by permission of the author.

Excerpts from *The Letters of William and Dorothy Wordsworth: The Early Years, 1787–1805*. Edited by Alan G. Hill, Mary Moorman, and Chester L. Shaver, copyright 1967 by Oxford University Press, used by permission of Oxford University Press.

Excerpts from *The Letters of William and Dorothy Wordsworth: The Middle Years, Part I, 1806–1811*. Edited by E. de Selincourt. Revised edition edited by Mary Moorman, copyright 1969 by Oxford University Press, used by permission of Oxford University Press.

Excerpts from *The Letters of William and Dorothy Wordsworth: The Middle Years, Part II, 1812–1820*. Edited by E. de Selincourt. Revised edition edited by Mary Moorman and Alan G. Hill, copyright 1970 by Oxford University Press, used by permission of Oxford University Press.

Excerpts from *William Wordsworth*. The Major Authors. Edited by Stephen Gill, copyright 2000 by Stephen Gill, used by permission of Oxford University Press.

Excerpts from *The Grasmere and Alfoxden Journals*. Edited by Pamela Woof, copyright 2002 by Pamela Woof, used by permission of Oxford University Press.

Excerpts from *A Narrative Concerning George and Sarah Green of the Parish of Grasmere, Addressed to a Friend*. Edited by E. de Selincourt, copyright 1936 by Oxford University Press, used by permission of Oxford University Press.

Excerpts from *The Song of the Earth* by Jonathan Bate, pp. 13–14, 42, 76, 107, 148, 150, and 245, Cambridge, Mass.: Harvard University Press, Copyright 2000 by Jonathan Bate. Also reproduced with permission of Palgrave Macmillan in the UK.

"Floating Island at Hawkshead, An Incident in the schemes of Nature" by Dorothy Wordsworth, reproduced by permission of The Wordsworth Trust, Dove Cottage, Cumbria, England.

"Grasmere—A Fragment" by Dorothy Wordsworth, reprinted by permission of the Division of Rare and Manuscript Collections, Cornell University Library and The Wordsworth Trust, Dove Cottage, Cumbria, England.

"An address to a Child in a high wind" by Dorothy Wordsworth from the Coleorton Commonplace Book, reprinted by permission of The Pierpont Morgan Library and The Wordsworth Trust, Dove Cottage, Cumbria, England.

Introduction: Dorothy Wordsworth's Ecology

Except for a handful of poems, selected and unostentatiously incorporated into his own volumes by her brother William, Dorothy Wordsworth's writings remained unpublished until the late nineteenth century.[1] And yet she has always been celebrated for her acute powers of observation. "Her information various—her eye watchful in minutest observation of nature—and her taste a perfect electrometer—it bends, protrudes, and draws in, at subtlest beauties & most recondite faults" (*Collected Letters* I 330–31). Allowing for its specialized language (modern readers can be grateful for Richard Holmes's explanation that an electrometer is "a tiny piece of exquisite gold foil in a glass vacuum, responding to minute fluctuations of an external electrical charge" [154]), Coleridge's assessment remains our own. Dorothy's watchful eye draws us in, and her descriptions of nature—and people—are notable for their impassioned accuracy. Nevertheless, her place in literary studies remains paradoxical. For example, we are now in the curious position of knowing more about Dorothy and her work than her contemporaries did. How has this affected our perception of Dorothy Wordsworth? How has this affected how we read her work? These questions were the catalysts for the present consideration of Dorothy Wordsworth, and it is my belief that reading her work from an ecological perspective can help us avoid adopting too readily—but also help us engage with—critical points of view perhaps already threatening to become shibboleths as a result of this belated surfeit of knowledge.

"The widest definition of the subject of ecocriticism," Greg Garrard has recently posited, "is the study of the relationship of the human and the non-human, throughout human cultural history and entailing critical analysis of the term 'human' itself" (5).[2] The present study focuses on Romantic cultural history in relation to predominantly rural environments, and its subject is a woman known for her radical self-effacement. It would not be an overstatement to say that Dorothy Wordsoworth's self-effacing tendencies have shaped virtually all criticism devoted to her, but in the present context I am especially interested in one strand (not necessarily ecocritical) devoted to interpreting her relationship to the phenomenal world. It covers a broad spectrum of concerns—from Dorothy's writing style to her identity as a woman living in her historical moment; and in fact I would like to approach my argument by quoting—and eventually discussing—two pointed statements that will take us from one end of this spectrum to the other. The first comes from Robert Gittings and Jo Manton's biography and involves their analysis of the Alfoxden journal, Dorothy's first formal attempt at writing. After a consideration of its opening entries, the first of which begins matter-of-factly with "[t]he green paths down the hillsides are channels for streams" (141),[3] and which is also notable for its avoidance of the first-person pronoun, Gittings and Manton suggest that the

> paradox of her unique style is that it is no style. The Alfoxton entries are practically in note-form. Nothing distracts. The acute observation by Dorothy is there, but no Dorothy herself. Every object, sight, sound is allowed its own nature. A warm day is built from a series of little impressions, matter-of-fact but cumulative. (77)

The second statement, from Anne K. Mellor's *Romanticism and Gender*, approaches Dorothy's identity as a woman living and writing in the late-eighteenth and into the nineteenth century through metaphorical extension, arguing that her late poem "Floating Island at Hawkshead"

> affirms a floating island life or self that is interactive, absorptive, constantly changing, and domestic—it can be contained within a tiny room. It is a self that produces and supports other lives—warbling birds, blooming flowers, a "crest of trees"—a self that provides food, shelter, safety for others. It is a self that is sometimes visible, sometimes not, a self that can appear and disappear in a moment, a self that is constructed in part—but only in part—by the gaze of others. . . . It is a self that is profoundly connected to its environment, to those "harmonious powers" of sunshine and storm, of nature and human society, that surround it, direct it, even consume it. . . . Significantly, it is a self that *does not name itself as a self*. . . . (156)[4]

Even if we disagree with Richard Fadem's contention that Dorothy's work is not "in any sustained way interesting as literature" (17), her writings still pose problems for her readers. There is the obvious fact that she is best known for her journals (in a period known for its poetry) and that until relatively recently critics had not really thought of interpreting them *as* journals. But we are now considering Dorothy's work for what it is rather than for what it is not, and I think we can trust that this will continue to be the case.[5] I would argue instead, then, that the greatest impediment to a clear-sighted understanding of Dorothy's work remains Dorothy herself, although I also hope to show that this has occurred as a result of our own limited perception.

It seems that Dorothy either said nothing at all about her work or expressed her extreme dissatisfaction with it, and by extension herself. For many readers, her description of "[t]he moonshine like herrings in the water" remains one of her most startling tropes, an excellent example of her unique powers of expression (Grasmere journals 30). And yet, her equally memorable statement that " . . . I should detest the idea of setting myself up as an Author" perpetually threatens to undermine our sense of her linguistic capabilities.[6] We can of course choose to ignore such a potentially debilitating binary—we can, that is, simply ignore Dorothy's self-denigrating pronouncements and instead extract and then distill those fragments of flashing brilliance into a satisfying aesthetic whole.[7] But this would be to ignore one of the most fascinating—and sometimes troubling—aspects of Dorothy's life and work: her relationship to the world she inhabited. As we have already seen, Gittings and Manton as well as Mellor examine this relationship, and I would now like to consider a little more closely the implications of their findings.

John Worthen states succinctly that with the Alfoxden journal "Dorothy was writing a diary of the world outside" (52). He makes a convincing argument for exactly why she may have felt compelled to keep a "nature journal" (53), his findings suggesting that her first formal work was an experiment.[8] This, then, might explain why, as Kenneth Johnston has pointed out, "there is hardly a single reference to public society in it" (*Hidden* 551).[9] It might also explain the journal's conspicuous absence of the first-person pronoun; consciously experimenting with language, she set out to record as matter-of-factly as possible (but also as sensitively as an "electrometer") what she saw, until work on what was to become *Lyrical Ballads* took her in another direction.[10] Gittings and Manton's analysis of Dorothy's style implicitly links its formation to the journal's experimental design, but what happens if we extend the range of the experiment to include everything she wrote?[11] For example, while Susan Levin clearly bases the following generalization on an intimate knowledge of Dorothy's entire written output, it results in a curiously circumscribed view of Dorothy herself, almost as if she had allowed herself to concentrate a little too closely on the Alfoxden journal's opening entries while simultaneously considering Dorothy's tendency to "put herself down":

> Her writing exists as a positive articulation of a negative situation. It is writing characterized by refusal: refusal to generalize, refusal to move out of a limited range of vision, refusal to speculate, refusal to reproduce standard literary forms, refusal to undertake the act of writing. . . . Her writing does not engage the world in the usual manner. She often appears a mere cataloguer of irrelevant detail, a person strangely fixed on the minutiae around her. (4)[12]

Levin limits her description of Dorothy's "refusals" to the act of writing; she broadens her argument, however, as she considers the pattern of Dorothy's life as it unfolds—and eventually unravels—in a natural environment that from an ecological perspective might sustain her: "To maintain herself in the natural world of Grasmere as well as in its authorial community she needs to write. Ultimately, however, Dorothy finds little space within the field of language offered and experiences a breakdown of mind and voice" (7). The causal chain Levin fashions here is compelling; however, we should be wary of arguments that link Dorothy's breakdown in health to her identity as a writer.[13] Gittings and Manton's research suggests that the origins of Dorothy's illness were physiological rather than professional or psychological (although it is of course true that her illness manifested itself psychologically as well).[14] But even more troubling, at least from an ecological perspective, is Levin's tendency to interpret Dorothy's work too exclusively within a human context. She acknowledges that "Grasmere was first of all a community of men and women in nature" (6), but her description of Dorothy's tragic fate (a problematic teleology in my opinion) betrays her greater interest in Grasmere as a "community of language" (6). Levin's account of "nature" in relation to Dorothy and her work, then, might in fact be more apparent than real. In a "community of language" it can only exist as a word.

Interestingly, Mellor's description of the female self as it emerges and disappears in continuous process in "Floating Island at Hawkshead," while clearly sharing the same foundation in feminist thought as that which informs Levin's analysis, takes us out of this prison-house of language.[15] Mellor's project—ultimately to "explore sensitively all the ways in which gender and sex intersect and complicate each other in particular Romantic texts" (4)—is very different from my own. That is, while I do—and indeed must—consider the role gender plays in Dorothy's life and work, I am finally most interested in examining (to quote from Garrard's definition again) the "relationship of the human and the non-human" as it manifests itself in them. Nevertheless, Mellor's sense of the female self as being "profoundly connected to its environment" represents a kind of incipient ecocriticism. In what follows I intend to expand thoroughly on what Mellor has only been able to imply. In doing so, we will be able to understand Dorothy's life and work not as a nexus of anxieties, which I would argue Levin's approach engenders, but as entities vitally connected to—and ultimately deriving their sustenance from—profoundly real natural environments.

"Is human consciousness part of nature?" Jonathan Bate poses this question toward the end of his revisionist reading of "Tintern Abbey" (*Song* 148). It possibly dodges the primary question of nature's ontological status (one that, as James McKusick has shown, influenced the course of Romantic ecology as it emerged in the early 1990s), but I would like to use it as a springboard for a consideration of the meagre role Dorothy has so far played in ecological studies of Romanticism.[16]

Bate answers his question as follows (I will leave his ecologically derived vocabulary undefined for the present as I consider it in the chapters that follow):

> Is human consciousness part of nature? For the picturesque theorist, it is not: the perceiving, dividing eye stands above and apart from its 'prospect.' That strand of environmentalism which emphasizes the conservation of landscapes of 'natural beauty' adopts the same stance. The converse position is that of Wordsworth's ecopoetic: 'the mind of man' can be a part of nature. 'Lines written a few miles above Tintern Abbey' offers not a *view* in the manner of the picturesque, but an exploration of the inter-relatedness of perception and creation, a meditation on the *networks* which link mental and environmental space. (148)

Bate's argument grows out of his cleverly linking "Tintern Abbey" to William's recriminatory analysis of his younger self's preoccupation with the picturesque in Book 11 of *The Prelude*.[17] In Bate's view, that Book's "twin critique of the picturesque and of Cartesianism" acts as a "gloss or commentary upon the poem that concludes the first volume of *Lyrical Ballads*" (142). Thus, his reading of "Tintern Abbey" concludes a chapter that locates the foundations of the "deep ecology" movement in William's rejection of the picturesque, and ultimately Descartes.

Any complete reading of the poem, however, must acknowledge Dorothy's role in it, and Bate concludes his interpretation by doing just that. He approaches this aspect of the poem once again via Book 11, this time by first examining William's pronouncements related to Mary, his future wife. There, we remember, William considers Mary's special relationship to nature:

> Whatever scene was present to her eyes,
> That was the best, to that she was attuned
> Through her humility and lowliness,
> And through a perfect happiness of soul
> Whose variegated feelings were in this
> Sisters, that they were each some new delight:
> For she was Nature's inmate. (208–14)[18]

William's beautiful tribute moves Bate into ecofeminist terrain, and his inclusion of Dorothy within it is crucial for my argument, which is why I must quote at length:

> Not mastery, then, but sisterhood; not the arrogance of enlighten-
> ment, but the humility of dwelling. [In Book 11 of *The Prelude*]
> Wordsworth proposes that it is women who are wise in matters eco-
> logical. Picturesque *feeling for* nature can only occur when one stands
> in the position of the spectator looking out or down upon an envi-
> ronment. Tourism thus shares industry's instrumental attitude towards
> nature. Whereas the tourist is a traveller, an outsider, the attuned and
> nurturing woman, Wordsworth suggests, is a dweller, an 'inmate' who
> *feels with* nature.
>
> The same move is made towards the end of 'Lines written a few
> miles above Tintern Abbey.' Woman—in *The Prelude* his wife Mary,
> in 'Lines' his sister Dorothy—is the power which draws man back to
> integration with nature. (150)

Bate's interpretation of William's depiction of humble but powerful women—Mary and then Dorothy—integrating the male poet back into nature represents the heart of his argument, and he is prepared for the response it might elicit:

> Orthodox feminists would say that to praise woman thus is to con-
> descend to her, to strip her of reason and speech, to entrap her. Does
> not 'inmate' suggest a prison cell? Ecofeminists would reply that the
> supposedly higher faculties which woman is here denied are precisely

those Cartesian presumptions with which we must do away if we are
to save the earth. (150)

In his earlier ecocritical study *Romantic Ecology: Wordsworth and the
Environmental Tradition*, Bate suggests that "in some readings . . . the
critic's purposes are also the writer's, and when this is the case there can be
a communion between living reader and dead writer which may bring with
it a particular enjoyment and a perception about endurance" (5). While he
might be working on a different level in *The Song of the Earth* (since its focus
extends well beyond the territory of the Lake District and William Wordsworth), Bate continues this communal reading process in his approach to
"Tintern Abbey," and that creates a problem. That is to say, while Bate's reading makes splendid ecocritical sense of William's poem, perhaps even allowing us a rare kind of communion with poet and work in the process, it finally
reveals very little about Dorothy Wordsworth herself. In fact, Bate's reading
of "Tintern Abbey" depends on his keeping her safely in the distance; we are
only allowed to perceive her through William's eyes. Granted, Bate guides
his reader through opposing feminist points of view and thus makes us *feel*
as though we are seeing the world as she saw it. A simple, disruptive truth
remains, however, as John Nabholtz pointed out long ago: "the picturesque
tradition was central to Dorothy's observation of landscape and was a con-
trolling principle in the natural descriptions found in her letters and journals"
(119). In other words, Nabholtz's findings support the idea that Dorothy did
not follow her brother in his (potentially) conscious rejection of Cartesianism, which in turn reveals the shaky foundation of Bate's ecofeminist reading
of William's poem. For it seems that a worshipper of the picturesque was
responsible for integrating him back into nature.

Bate's silencing of Dorothy in his reading of "Tintern Abbey" cannot
by itself explain her near absence of presence in the other major ecocritical studies of Romanticism that have so far appeared, but it is nevertheless
instructive. For example, it illustrates that Dorothy cannot necessarily be
read from an ecofeminist point of view without her brother's support and
that it is precisely that support that threatens to distort both figures. Reading
Dorothy ecologically entails a holistic approach, one that can account for
those aspects of her identity perhaps least attractive to current green thinkers,
such as her devotion to the picturesque. At the same time, though, and as I
hope to demonstrate in the chapters that follow, reading Dorothy's work ecologically might very well alter our sense of the foundations of that devotion.

Why do Jonathan Bate, Karl Kroeber, and James McKusick—to name
three of the most prominent ecocritics of Romanticism to have emerged

since the 1990s—all but ignore Dorothy?[19] The causes of this neglect are of course probably multifarious, although it is interesting to discover that these critics tend to mention her only in relation to William's most famous poem, "Tintern Abbey." Perhaps keeping Dorothy in the background ensures that she and William will emerge from an ecological investigation with their pristine images intact as nature worshippers uncannily prescient of our current standards? It is also possible that these critics have simply fallen under the spell of those contemporary figures, such as Coleridge, who tended to idealize her. Whatever the ultimate cause, we do both William and Dorothy a disservice by not considering more closely the role she played in shaping an environmental awareness that has its origins in the nineteenth century.

Before briefly describing the contents of the following four chapters, I would like to offer an entry from the Alfoxden journal as a kind of initial guide for reading Dorothy's work ecologically. Like most of its other entries, this one describes a walk out into nature—a departure and return:

> *February 1ˢᵗ* [1798]. About two hours before dinner, set forward towards Mr Bartelmy's. The wind blew so keen in our faces that we felt ourselves inclined to seek the covert of the wood. There we had a warm shelter, gathered a burthen of large rotten boughs blown down by the wind of the preceding night. The sun shone clear, but all at once a heavy blackness hung over the sea. The trees almost *roared*, and the ground seemed in motion with the multitudes of dancing leaves, which made a rustling sound distinct from that of the trees. Still the asses pastured in quietness under the hollies, undisturbed by these forerunners of the storm. The wind beat furiously against us when we returned. Full moon. She rose in uncommon majesty over the sea, slowly ascending through the clouds. Sat with the window open an hour in the moonlight. (143–44)

Pamela Woof's note for the entry informs us that "Mr Bartelmy," or John Bartholomew, "was bailiff for the St Albyn family who owned Alfoxden" (281), so presumably Dorothy and her brother had some business to attend to that evening. Of course, her use of "we" might indicate more than one companion, but we happen to know that Coleridge, their most frequent walking companion at that time, was away, so it is likely brother and sister braved the elements alone together. In any event, her use of the first-person plural deflects attention away from herself, perhaps giving her a greater freedom to describe what she saw. The entry, however, also moves beyond—without ever completely leaving—the visual realm, and in fact it unfolds as a series of kinetic contrasts. The wind blows "keen in their faces," so they find a "warm shelter" and rest. While in this shelter, however, Dorothy also gathers a "burthen of large rotten boughs blown down by the wind of the preceding night." (Here, we might notice Dorothy's habitual restlessness—she preferred to be engaged in useful activity.) Her keen eye for detail still intact (the boughs she gathers are "rotten"), she describes the "asses pastured in quietness under the hollies, undisturbed by these forerunners of the storm," a quietly haunting distillation of the kinetic contrasts driving the entire passage that momentarily takes her into a non-human realm. Perhaps somewhat conventionally (or humanistically), however, the entry concludes indoors—"Sat with the window open in the moonlight." That moonlight emerges as the dominant image of the entry, and indeed of the entire journal, serving to illuminate the full range of Dorothy's experience of nature; for the attentive reader will have noticed that the entry is finally both kinetically and aesthetically organized.[20] Dorothy goes out into nature. She walks, works, and sometimes even experiences complete communion with non-human existence. But she also reposes and looks. (The frame of the open window is like the canvas of the painter of picturesque landscapes). If we wish to experience Dorothy's work as a totality, we must strive to balance her kinetic and aesthetic sides.

The breakdown of the book is as follows. Chapter 1 introduces perhaps the most fundamental concept of ecology through a paradigmatic reading of Dorothy's best-known work, the Grasmere journals. Haphazardly assembled, even ending abruptly in mid-sentence, the journals Dorothy dedicated to the recording of their daily life in Grasmere, in four separate notebooks, nevertheless accrete to form an ecosystem, a delicate web of individual entries existing in interrelationship with one another. The chapter builds to an analysis of perhaps Dorothy's most famous journal entry—her description of the daffodils. Chapter 2 considers Dorothy as a simultaneous dweller and tourist through an examination of her *Recollections of a Tour Made in Scotland*. Written between 1803 and 1805, Dorothy's travel journal allows us to perceive the relationship between tourism and environmentalism as Dorothy reflects (in writing, from the vantage point of her home in Grasmere) on her experiences in a "wild," foreign country. In this chapter I argue that tourism and ecology are ultimately interrelated practices—unique manifestations occurring as a result of broader changes taking place in England and the Europe in the eighteenth and nineteenth centuries.[21] Chapter 3 is devoted to Dorothy's poetry—more precisely, her ecopoetry. It begins by imagining the scene of writing as a means of establishing her identify as an ecopoet and then moves into close readings of three of Dorothy's poems, "An address to a Child in a high wind," "Grasmere—A Fragment," and "Floating Island at Hawkshead." This chapter seeks to establish a viable model for an examination of Dorothy's other poems, thus quietly rejecting the idea that she was not a poet worthy of our consideration. Chapter 4 examines Dorothy's relationship with the dead. In some ways almost wholly preoccupied with the human realm, this chapter nevertheless seeks to establish a connection between Dorothy's participation in a culture of death and her daily experiences in the natural world. The chapter is organized around a close reading of one of Dorothy's lesser-known works, *A Narrative Concerning George and Sarah Green of the Parish of Grasmere*. The Conclusion considers a few of the key ideas explored here from a slightly different angle.

Chapter One

Bringing It All Back Home:
The Ecology of Dorothy Wordsworth's
Grasmere Journals

Perhaps no one has thought as long or as deeply about William Wordsworth's "Home at Grasmere" as Karl Kroeber. And what ties this thought together conceptually is an interest in ecology. From "'Home at Grasmere': Ecological Holiness" (1974) to *Ecological Literary Criticism: Romantic Imagining and the Biology of Mind* (1994), Kroeber has consistently explored what is surely one of William's most problematic long poems in relation to matters of the earth. This is fitting given that "Home at Grasmere" is William's paean (really a kind of sustained crescendo) to a cherished spot, a spot the poet early on in the poem rather audaciously describes as

> A termination, and a last retreat,
> A Centre, come from wheresoe'er you will,
> A Whole without dependence or defect,
> Made for itself, and happy in itself,
> Perfect Contentment, Unity entire. (166–70)

In fact, it is precisely this passage that Kroeber seizes upon, ultimately arguing that this "Unity entire" represents nothing less than a complex ecosystem. He elucidates this fundamental ecological concept through a methodology that mirrors the concept he describes, which is to say that, for Kroeber, an ecosystem explains William's poem to the same degree that William's poem explains the concept of an ecosystem. This gives his discussions of "Home at Grasmere" an unusual breadth and allows him to introduce ecological ideas to a more "purely" literary-oriented audience.

Take the following example for instance, which comes from the aforementioned *Ecological Literary Criticism*. "An ecosystem," Kroeber writes, "is a constantly self-transforming continuity. No ecosystem exists outside time or is adequately representable as anything other than an encompassing ongoing process made up of diversely intersecting subordinate temporal processes" (55). This definition occurs in the context of Kroeber's discussion of "Home at Grasmere," and it neatly illustrates his desire to take us inside and out-side Romantic poems at one and the same time. After all, what makes an ecosystem an ecosystem is the idea of interconnectedness, and in Kroeber's view "Home at Grasmere" represents only one example (but a very signifi-cant one) of the interconnectedness of everything on the earth, whether it be works of literature shaped by the hands of men and women or flowers conditioned to grow in greenhouses.

But if everything really is intimately interconnected in an ecosystem, then so are works of literature and the writers who produce them. And who were more interconnected in life and in literature (no matter how one-sided that connection might seem) than William and Dorothy Word-sworth? Even enforced separation could not threaten this relationship, as Dorothy herself articulates in a letter to her lifelong friend, Jane Pollard, where she says that she and her brothers

> have been endeared to each other by early misfortune. We in the same
> moment lost a father, a mother, a home, we have been equally deprived
> of our patrimony by the cruel Hand of lordly Tyranny. . . . Neither
> absence nor Distance nor Time can ever break the chain that links me
> to my Brothers. (*Early Years* 88)

Dorothy wrote this in February of 1793, a full year before she and Wil-liam—the brother to whom she ultimately felt closest—would be reunited, never to part again. Of course, nothing could alter their status as orphans, but they would regain the home (and eventually claim the "patrimony") they had lost when they were children. And if they were remarkably unset-tled initially, living at Windy Brow, Racedown, Alfoxden, and even in Ger-many between the years 1794 and 1799, they finally settled for life back in their beloved Lake District—in Grasmere to be more precise—at the very end of 1799.

"Home at Grasmere" celebrates this homecoming, and, as Jonathan Wordsworth has argued, it "is, almost in its entirety, a poem of 1800" (28).[1] The Grasmere journals, Dorothy Wordsworth's most famous writings, are also works of 1800—at least initially. Unlike William's poem, however, no controversy surrounds the composition and completion of Dorothy's jour-nals, simply because precise dates are a generic attribute of journals them-selves. They move patiently through time (beginning on May 14, 1800) and end abruptly—in mid-sentence—on January 16, 1803. Meanwhile, it would seem that "Home at Grasmere" attempts to perpetuate the year 1800 through a kind of endless circular movement, which might at least partially explain why scholars have disputed the composition and completion of the poem.[2] In spite of their radical differences, then (and, indeed, in spite of their very different approaches to subject matter in general), "Home at Grasmere" and the Grasmere journals are preoccupied with time. More precisely, they are preoccupied with the relationship between time and space, since both works grow out of and respond to a dearly beloved place: Grasmere. Karl Kroeber's ecological reading of William's poem illuminates the subtle relationship between time and space in both works and in doing so paves the way for our understanding of the Grasmere journals themselves as a kind of unique ecosystem.

A good place to begin is with part of an entry near the end of the journals. Dorothy and William have been away for most of the summer; they have been to France (where Dorothy met Annette Vallon, William's former lover, and their illegitimate daughter, Caroline), and they are now, in October of 1802, making the journey back to Grasmere. Accompanying them is Mary Wordsworth, William's new wife.

> A shower came on just after we left the Inn while the Rain beat against the Windows we ate our dinners which M & W heartily enjoyed—I was not quite well. When we passed thro' the village of Wensly my heart was melted away with dear recollections, the Bridge, the little waterspout the steep hill the Church—They are among the most vivid of my own inner visions, for they were the first objects that I saw after we were left to ourselves, & had turned our whole hearts to Grasmere as a home in which we were to rest. The Vale looked most beautiful each way. . . . I could not help observing as we went along how much more *varied* the prospects of Wensly Dale are in the summer time than I could have thought possible in the winter. (129)

This entry concludes very precisely several pages later with Dorothy commemorating a significant occasion: "On Friday 8th we baked Bread, & Mary & I walked, first upon the Hill side, & then in John's Grove, then in view of Rydale, the first walk that I had taken with my Sister" (132). The placidity of this final sentence (a miniature entry in itself) is all the more striking for its appearance at the end of an entry overflowing with barely contained emotion. Dorothy's chaotic journey through England, then to France, and then through England again comes to an end as she and her new sister take measured steps in a familiar landscape.

Reading this entry in relation to other entries, and at the same time limiting our angle of vision, we begin to detect a pattern, one that allows us to find order in an otherwise sprawling, disorganized body of writings. Emotional haste informs the entry preceding their departure for France: "The Swallows I must leave them the well the garden the Roses all—Dear creatures!! they sang last night after I was in bed—seemed to be singing to one another, just before they settled to rest for the night. Well I must go— Farewell.————. " (119). According to Pamela Woof, Dorothy's "handwriting becomes larger and looser as the moment to leave approaches and she continues to write" (244). Clearly Dorothy is writing during a moment of intense emotion (not one, but two exclamation marks), but she manages to maintain composure, for as Woof goes on to point out, she "still manages to insert the extra word 'white' to describe the sky-like brightness of the lake" (244). And in fact, if we go back to the very first entry of the journals we notice that Dorothy's desire for equanimity seems to be her reason for writing in the first place: "I resolved to write a journal of the time till W[illiam] & J[ohn] return, & I set about keeping my resolve because I will not quarrel with myself, & because I shall give Wm Pleasure by it when he comes home again" (1). Quite simply, the Grasmere journals are an act of will; those measured steps she takes with her new sister "first upon the Hill side, & then in John's Grove, then in view of Rydale" have been hard won. Kenneth Johnston puts it succinctly when he suggests that "[t]hese are the diary entries of a woman whose heart is breaking but who is determined not to lose her mind under the strain" (*Hidden* 715).

Johnston's statement takes us into a kind of psychic landscape. Similarly, by emphasizing Dorothy's will to write we have emphasized the interiority of the journals. The physical landscape Dorothy has become famous for describing recedes somewhat as we discover her need for psychic containment, a need that might mirror our own rage for order as readers. Susan Levin claims that "[i]f we wish to find a narrative structure for this text, we may say it is Dorothy's story of William's engagement and marriage to Mary Hutchinson" (21). The passage with which I opened my examination of the Grasmere journals occurs at the end of this "narrative structure" and represents the end of the story: Mary Hutchinson has become Mary Wordsworth. From a logical perspective, then, it makes sense that the journals themselves should come to an end shortly thereafter. But does this narrative of psychic containment represent the whole story? Elsewhere, Woof suggests the existence of several narratives in the Grasmere journals (for example, "the story of Coleridge, his excited coming to the Lake District, a stranger to it, and then his depression. . . ."), but then points out that as "interesting as they are as they mingle together, they do not explain the ultimate fineness of the journal" ("Dorothy" 160–61). She proceeds to eschew a narrative approach in favour of a close analysis of Dorothy's remarkable powers of description. For many of us, those remarkable powers represent the genuine Dorothy Wordsworth, and yet the journals' many narratives (which possibly mingle together to form a kind of grand narrative, according to Susan Levin and others) are not necessarily going to go away.[3] Is there a way to read the Grasmere journals that accounts for these intersecting modes of writing, one that will transform our understanding of Dorothy's relationship to her world—and deliver that world as a palpable presence—in the process?

In order to approach this question, we need to return to Karl Kroeber's definition of an ecosystem, but with the word "journal" replacing "ecosystem":

> [A journal] is a constantly self-transforming continuity. No [journal] exists outside time or is adequately representable as anything other than an encompassing ongoing process made up of diversely intersecting subordinate temporal processes. (55)

On one level, such an alteration might seem no more than a bit of semantic trickery—and besides, we can look elsewhere for definitions of journals. Robert A. Fothergill, for example, claims that a diary (he notes the "shadowy difference" between a diary and a journal and thus uses the two words more or less interchangeably) "articulates the subject matter of one day at a time" (82, 84). Since both Fothergill's and Kroeber's definitions revolve around concepts of time, and precisely this link suggests that, the Grasmere journals illustrate what both definitions, with a nudge from the enterprising reader, work together to suggest: that there is an ecology of journal writing.

As I have already pointed out, the Grasmere journals move through time, which suggests a linear process. We need look no further than those dated, sequential entries for proof of this, and it seems that any narrative approach to the journals works from this linear perspective, since all good stories (at least of a certain kind) have beginnings, middles, and ends. But the journals end with a dash, not a period—that is, they do not actually end, but simply trail off, rather like an unresolved note of music left to fade quietly in the air. We ourselves round off the journals; we bring them to an end, typically through speculation as to why exactly she "stopped" writing. Robert Gittings and Jo Manton have engaged in precisely this kind of speculation.

> It is often asked why Dorothy ceased to keep her Grasmere journal after
> 16 January, in spite of determining to start a new book and 'write regu-
> larly and, if I can, legibly' [Grasmere journals 137]. Some unlikely rea-
> sons have been put forward; the most likely is that now, in spite of her
> resolve, she simply did not have time." (142–43)

Gittings and Manton's speculations are quite sensible; Dorothy was certainly
busy looking after a new household and a pregnant sister-in-law. But we should
not press this too far, since the journals themselves illustrate how little time
Dorothy ever had for writing.[4] Moreover, the fact that "unlikely reasons have
been put forward" suggests that we cannot really know why Dorothy stopped
keeping a journal at this time. And she certainly did not stop writing. Letters
continued to flow from the cottage at Town End (compared to her brother,
Dorothy was much more assiduous about letter writing), and of course she
would keep journals again, some of them quite extensive.[5] My feeling here
is that when faced with the cessation of the journals, our need to read them
as an extended narrative takes precedence. Gittings and Manton's speculations fit nicely into that grand narrative Susan Levin locates, for they point out
(immediately after musing on why Dorothy failed to return to the journals)
that supporting Mary "in the second half of her pregnancy was a prospect she
embraced with the whole of her loving feelings" (143). This is true, but it does
not necessarily have anything to do with Dorothy's writing habits; rather, we
make the connection and then follow it to its logical conclusion.

   I do not mean to belabour our tendency to read Dorothy's journals for
the presence of narratives; nor do I doubt the existence of those narratives
(although I would—and will—question the presence of an all-encompassing
narrative in the Grasmere journals). They exist, however, within an altogether
larger framework, and Susan Levin herself hints at this when she describes the
paradoxical nature of Dorothy's journals:

> The journals are not a simple series of happenings; events are emplotted
> and through a sequence make various statements about the emotional
> life of the narrator. At the same time, however, as the journals contain
> the open-endedness of the form (journal as day-by-day, indefinitely con-
> tinuous account), they also each seem to tell a story that can be read as
> an enclosed narrative: the story of William's marrying in the Grasmere
> journal or the story of a particular trip in the travel journals. (8)

Levin's point that Dorothy's journals can be read either as open forms or
as an enclosed narrative uncannily resembles Kroeber's definition of an

ecosystem as a "constantly self-transforming continuity." One of the most fascinating aspects of examining the Grasmere journals from an ecological perspective is our discovery that a wide range of recent literary criticism helps explain the journals' ecological processes without actually knowing that it is doing so. Fothergill and Levin are not concerned with ecological matters, and Kroeber mentions Dorothy only once (and then only in relation to Dorothy's role in "Tintern Abbey"), and yet, taken collectively, their ideas inform our awareness of the ecology of Dorothy's work. This might suggest the amorphousness of ecologically oriented thought; however, it ultimately illustrates the elusiveness of the journals themselves. They so naturally accrete to form an ecosystem that we are scarcely aware of it.

The Grasmere journals are more than linear constructs, then (and yet, they are at least in part linear constructs; embracing the paradoxical is the key to comprehending Dorothy's journals), but what else are they? In his most recent ecologically oriented study, *The Song of the Earth*, Jonathan Bate argues that "an ecosystem does not have a centre" but instead is comprised of a "network of relations" (107). Bate's statement reminds us that ecosystems not only exist temporally but are also spatial entities, albeit of a particular kind. Time and space are of course crucial to the Grasmere journals (we have decided to call them the *Grasmere* journals after all), and I would like to consider their relationship in Dorothy's work by revisiting the entry with which I began my examination.

Woof speculates that after Dorothy's departure in July "much of the Journal is recollected narrative" and suggests that she might not have composed this material until the last week of October, when she "had been 'confined upstairs' for a week 'in the tooth ache'" (Grasmere journals xviii-xix). In other words, Dorothy writes from the "Centre" of Grasmere. She recalls all that she has seen, all that she has experienced (or rather, what she prefers to recall), her journal acting as the living medium through which that experience is refracted. I say "living" because Dorothy's engagement with her recent past ultimately represents a new experience as separate "spots of time" collapse into one another:

> When we passed thro' the village of Wensly my heart was melted away with dear recollections, the Bridge, the little waterspout the steep hill the Church—They are among the most vivid of my own inner visions, for they were the first objects that I saw after we were left to ourselves, & had turned our whole hearts to Grasmere as a home in which we were to rest. (129)

An emotional interfusion occurs here captured in the prose itself by the grad-
ual disappearance of punctuation in that first clause, Dorothy recalling in the
present moment of writing her distant and more recent pasts. All of this is,
of course, perfectly Wordsworthian (hence my use of William's terminology);
however, we look in vain for an exact analogue to Dorothy's experiences in
William's descriptions of a distinctly poetic process. For in keeping a journal,
Dorothy merges domestic and natural spaces, and it is here that we approach
the genuinely Dorothy Wordsworthian.

   If the above example represents emotion recollected in tranquility, we
must not forget Dorothy's fondness for the tranquility of the present moment.
Again and again (and this might distinguish the Grasmere journals from her
other work), Dorothy captures experience in the moment of writing. And if
the results seem less philosophically complicated than the work that sprung
from William's theories of poetry (or was it the other way around?), these
entries nevertheless possess an attractive immediacy rarely found in other
writing contexts. Here is one example: "*Saturday January 30ʰ* [1802]: A cold
dark morning. William chopped wood—I brought it in in a basket—a cold
wind—Wm slept better but he thinks he looks ill—he is shaving now" (60).
And here is another (a portion of the entry for Tuesday, March 23, 1802):
"[I]t is about 10 o clock, a quiet night. The fire flutters & the watch ticks
I hear nothing else save the Breathings of my Beloved & he now & then
pushes his book forward & turns over a leaf. Fletcher is not come home. No
letter from C" (82). In their quiet intimacy, these entries seem to place the
reader in the middle of a keenly felt domestic environment, which might
in part explain why the Grasmere journals (by far Dorothy's most popular
writings) have been attracting admirers for over a century. Instead of theory,
or argument, or even traditional narrative, Dorothy offers us the quiet dyna-
mism of the living moment.

   Knowledgeable readers also realize, however, to what extent William's
presence contributes to this domestic tranquility; for, as we have already
seen, his absence affects Dorothy rather differently. "Oh! that I had a letter
from William!" she exclaims at the end of her first entry—only hours after
he and John have left the cottage at Town End (2). Such an outburst invites
a psychological interpretation, and we need not deny Johnston's feeling that
Dorothy begins her journal as a kind of therapy, particularly since Dorothy
herself more or less states this. But perhaps we have attended more to the
cause than the effects of the psychological dynamic that impels the journals
into being? For if it is true that Dorothy experiences angst with William's frequent comings and goings, she also works hard at recalling his presence while
he is away, the result being a heightened—and for us glorious—awareness

of her surroundings. I am not suggesting that, either present or absent, William is the sole cause of Dorothy's remarkable powers of perception, for her powers are hers and hers alone; rather, I wish to underscore the human—and by extension domestic—foundations of that perception. Appreciating this relationship ultimately affects our sense of how Dorothy writes Grasmere as ecosystem.

It also allows us to make sense of a series of contradictions. I use Wordsworthian language in claiming that Dorothy writes from the "Centre" of Grasmere, while Bate believes that an ecosystem is centreless. Meanwhile, Kroeber argues that Grasmere Vale is an ecosystem precisely because of that "Centre." Now, if we cannot quite "pass . . . unalarmed" this labyrinth of contradictions (to borrow language from the great Prospectus itself ["Home at Grasmere" 984]), we can nevertheless begin to work our way through it—as soon, that is, as we realize that Dorothy's deep understanding of the domestic and natural worlds gives her a unique vantage point from which to work. She writes from the "Centre" of Grasmere (symbolically represented by the cottage at Town End) and in the process captures its existence as a "network of relations." This means that Dorothy inhabits a somewhat paradoxical space (perhaps hardly surprising given that she was a woman writing at the beginning of the nineteenth century and the sister of William Wordsworth). Her unique position also, however, lends her work a remarkable—as well as a somewhat complicated—consistency, particularly at the level of language.

For Dorothy consistently describes a peopled landscape. In fact, the word "peopled" itself seems to have formed a cornerstone of Dorothy's always-developing landscape lexicon. She did not, however, use language as a substitute for a Claude glass. That is to say, while Dorothy did, like any writer of her time interested in the picturesque, tend to frame nature linguistically in such a way as to suggest a picture, she nevertheless always made humans a part of that frame.[6] Dorothy's use of the word "peopled" illustrates this, appearing in its varying forms on at least two occasions in her work before and after she kept her Grasmere journals. More important, in both instances Dorothy uses the word expressly to capture features of the landscape, but with contrasting results.

The word first appears in the Alfoxden journal, but even here (in the first entry of Dorothy's first-ever journal) we might argue that Dorothy bends the picturesque frame:

Alfoxden, 20ᵗʰ January 1798. The green paths down the hill-sides are channels for streams. The young wheat is streaked by silver lines of

water running between the ridges, the sheep are gathered together on
the slopes. After the wet dark days, the country seems more populous. It
peoples itself in the sunbeams. The garden, mimic of spring, is gay with
flowers. (141)

Tackling Robert Con Davis' claim that humans tend to become "discrete
shadows" in Dorothy's work (Davis forwarding an argument familiar to
students of the picturesque[7]), Robert Mellin (discussing this same entry)
counters that humans "aren't 'absent' in the foliage, but are represented as
integrated into their surroundings, a nonanthropocentric representation
of humans that seems increasingly useful to twentieth-century environmental writers" (73). Dorothy appears to confound our ecological expec-
tations, however, when she re-introduces the word in the fourth stanza of
her excellent late poem, "Floating Island at Hawkshead":

> Food, shelter, safety there they find
> There berries ripen, flowerets bloom;
> There insects live their lives—and die:
> A peopled *world* it is;—in size a tiny room. (13–16)

Here, Dorothy makes sense of a peculiar natural phenomenon (" . . . a
slip of earth, / By throbbing waves long undermined, / Loosed from its
hold. . . ." [5–7]) through a simple comparison, likening the island to
"a tiny room." This domestic transformation allows both speaker and
reader, who are themselves presumably ensconced in comfortable rooms,
to absorb and understand the sometimes uncanny—as well as unremit-
ting—processes of nature. Taken together, these examples illustrate that
for Dorothy the human and natural worlds exist in beautiful interrelationship. Reading ecologically, then, allows us to perceive the harmony
of Dorothy's peopled descriptions of nature as apparent contradictions
retreat into the shadows.

Shifting our attention back to the Grasmere journals, we find that
they contain a similar—if differently inflected—harmonious vision. And
this becomes especially apparent when we turn to the entry containing
Dorothy's famous description of the daffodils. This passage is famous
for a variety of reasons, not least of which because the "little colony" of
flowers Dorothy describes eventually spring up on the shores of William's
imagination and bloom into a poem. We need to examine Dorothy's well-
known words—and so interdependent are they that reading fragments
will not do.

When we were in the woods beyond Gowbarrow park we saw a few daffodils close to the water side, we fancied that the lake had floated the seeds ashore & that the little colony had so sprung up—But as we went along there were more & yet more & at last under the boughs of the trees, we saw that there was a long belt of them along the shore, about the breadth of a country turnpike road. I never saw daffodils so beautiful they grew among the mossy stones about & about them, some rested their heads upon these stones as on a pillow for weariness & the rest tossed & reeled & danced & seemed as if they verily laughed with the wind that blew upon them over the Lake, they looked so gay ever glancing ever changing. This wind blew directly over the Lake to them. There was here & there a little knot & a few stragglers a few yards higher up but they were so few as not to disturb the simplicity & unity & life of that one busy highway. (85)

It is easy to see why this inspired William. Dorothy's precise diction and flexible prose rhythms (her lightly punctuated sentences contributing to this flexibility) combine to form an impressive whole. The steadily sweeping movement from "a few daffodils" to "the simplicity & unity & life of that one busy highway" might remind us of William's rising and falling blank verse rhythms. This is not a poem, however, and closer scrutiny of Dorothy's journal writing practices will reveal a different kind of unity in the making.

In her editorial notes for this entry, Woof points out that the clause "This wind blew directly over the Lake to [the daffodils]" is an "added insertion" and then asks us to compare Dorothy's

description of the walk along Ullswater in her letter to Mary, written immediately on returning home. . . . Though the wind there is 'furious' and 'sometimes almost took our breath away,' it is not a creative force: no daffodils are mentioned, no partnership with the wind in dance. (232)

We surmise that Dorothy wrote this entry after she wrote her letter to Mary. Moreover, Woof draws our attention to Dorothy's (William) Wordsworthian tendencies, since clearly she composed the entry and passage after the events of the day had settled in her imagination. The famous daffodils passage, then, is at bottom a creative transformation. And like William, Dorothy is particularly interested in capturing the process of this transformation. But where "I Wandered Lonely as a Cloud" depicts the activity of the poet's mind as an end in itself and invites us to share in it (or perhaps simply witness it), Dorothy's journal entry offers the act of the mind as part of a much more inclusive, ecological process. For in its totality the entry containing Dorothy's description of the daffodils captures the rising and falling rhythms of a single—and in most respects ordinary—day.

And like any ordinary day, this one was shaped by weather[8]:

> *Thursday [April] 15th*. It was a threatening misty morning—but mild. We set off after dinner from Eusemere—Mrs. Clarkson went a short way with us but turned back. The wind was furious & we thought we must have returned. We first rested in the large Boat-house, then under a furze Bush opposite Mr. Clarksons, saw the plow going in the field. The wind seized our breath the Lake was rough. (84–85)

Dorothy imports the adjective "furious" from her letter to Mary, and yet within a few sentences the "furious" wind becomes (to adopt William's famous language) a "mild creative breeze" (*The Prelude*, Book I 43). Such a transformation would seem almost miraculous (the wind seizing their breath representing an example of literal inspiration) were we simply to stop reading after her description of the daffodils. Keeping in mind, however, that this is, in fact, a recollected account, we might consider how the end of the day possibly coloured her perception of earlier events:

> —Rain came on, we were wet when we reached Luffs but we called in. Luckily all was chearless & gloomy so we faced the storm—we *must* have been wet if had waited—put on dry clothes at Dobson's. I was very kindly treated by a young woman, the Landlady looked sour but it is her way. She gave us a goodish supper, excellent ham and potatoes. We paid 7/ when we came away. William was sitting by a bright fire when I came downstairs he soon made his way to the Library piled up in the corner of the window. He brought out a volume of Enfield's Speaker, another miscellany, & an odd volume of Congreve's plays. We had a glass of warm rum & water—we enjoyed ourselves and wished for Mary. It rained & blew when we went to bed. (85–86)

Under a cloud of threatening weather the entire day, Dorothy and William only narrowly avoid a good soaking. Eventually, however, they find their way back to Dobson's (the Inn where they were staying), and from that point on (once they have changed out of their wet clothes, that is, for it seems they could not wholly avoid getting wet) a cheerful domestic glow suffuses the rest of the passage.

Good(ish) food, (more or less) pleasant accommodations, books, rum, conversation—the details here at the end of the entry return us in circular fashion back to the mildness Dorothy took note of at the beginning of the day, offering us a glimpse of the ecological vision that would fully bloom into existence as the century progressed.

"The word 'ecology' (*Oekologie*)," writes Bate, "was coined in 1866 by the German zoologist Ernst Haeckel and defined more fully by the same scientist in 1870: 'By ecology we mean the body of knowledge concerning the economy of nature—the investigation of the total relations of the animal both to its organic and to its inorganic environment. . . . '" (*Romantic* 36). In *Nature's Economy: A History of Ecological Ideas*, Donald Worster points out that "Haeckel derived the new label from the same root found in the older word 'economy': the Greek *oikos*, referring originally to the family household and its daily operations and maintenance" (192). Recently, ecologically oriented scholars (including Bate) have argued that, due to their special place in literary history, a surprising number of Romantic-period writers articulated key ideas we associate with the later development of ecology, thus making them "proto-ecologists." The entry containing Dorothy's description of the daffodils offers us one more compelling example of this phenomenon, although to my knowledge no one has examined it as such, possibly because of our tendency to uproot the daffodils from their contextual soil. Placing the daffodils back in the total environment of the entry itself, however, we discover that for Dorothy there is both an "economy of nature" (to quote Haeckel) and a domestic economy, a harmonious relationship that in fact beautifully anticipates Haeckel's neologism.

Which brings us back to the role memory plays in the construction of the entry. Obvious enough on one level (memory being the foundation on which journals are built), Dorothy's affinity for recollection nevertheless shapes her work in rather subtle ways. Of course, we know that she consistently—some would say pathologically—eschewed dwelling on herself in her writing (and we have already seen how this has influenced our desire to mine her work for its self-revelations in the form of covert narratives), which means that her memory worked centrifugally. Dorothy had a marvellous eye for detail, and this is especially apparent in this entry. But what do we *do* with this detail? Dorothy's richly poetic description of the daffodils occurs in an entry that concludes with the details of their evening meal, right down to its price. Granted, Woof informs us that Dorothy goes into even greater detail about this meal in her letter to Mary (232); however, she does not ignore it here. It seems that for Dorothy there is always a wealth—a surplus—of detail to account for, perhaps giving her work a slightly disorganized quality.[9]

Or perhaps Dorothy simply knew that the world she moved through—and was vitally connected to—was an "encompassing ongoing process" and that a true engagement with this world demanded a similar approach to writing? And here we might wish to remind ourselves of the most obviously "poetic" aspect of Dorothy's description of the daffodils—her simple but elegant use of pathetic fallacy. "I never saw daffodils so beautiful," she writes. They rest "their heads upon these stones as on a pillow" (85). They toss, and even dance. We know how these words affected William—and in fact the somewhat mysterious history of the imaginative events that resulted in "I Wandered Lonely as a Cloud" forms a cornerstone of (William) Wordsworthian criticism. But where gaps paradoxically lend substance to William's imaginative process (that is, the imaginative faculty, while central to creativity, remains opaque, essentially unknowable), Dorothy's approach to writing is especially notable for its utter straightforwardness. Put another way, Dorothy's fascination with the details of everyday existence means that the imaginative steps she takes in transforming nature form an active part of her descriptive process. This only becomes clear, however, when we examine journal entries as totalities, as little interrelated worlds in themselves. We recall, for example, Dorothy's careful description of the domestic scene that ends this memorable day. Seemingly superfluous, these details nevertheless paradoxically look forward to Dorothy's description of the daffodils. That is to say, if we can imagine Dorothy recalling the total experience of the day from the "Centre" of the cottage at Town End, we can also imagine her extending in backwards fashion the glow of the domestic interior at Dobson's to the daffodils themselves. The little flowers seem to depend on a kind of human solar system for their existence.

Interpreted thus, the daffodils are poised to spring forth as a full-blown metaphor for human community, and yet they remain firmly rooted in the soil of their natural environment. Uniquely themselves, then, the daffodils are also examples of pure potential, and this is only fitting given that Dorothy's depiction of the flowers occurs within the Grasmere journals. Haphazardly assembled, temporally erratic (they begin as abruptly as they end), the four separate notebooks that Dorothy casually but also carefully maintained have nevertheless sprung up in our imaginations as a whole (indeed, they are sometimes understandably but mistakenly referred to as the Grasmere *journal*). Why is this? To answer this question we need to turn back (circular movement having formed the leitmotif of this chapter) to the work with which we began—"Home at Grasmere."

To a certain extent, "Home at Grasmere" is a work of the late nineteenth century in that it did not begin its public life until 1888, when it was published (curiously enough) as *The Recluse*. Interestingly, the same holds true for the Grasmere journals, William Knight overseeing their publication (in somewhat expurgated form) nearly ten years later in 1897. Of course, the posthumous publication of literary works follows its own wayward rules, which means that we should avoid reductive speculations; nevertheless, I find this delay in publication fascinating, especially in relation to the ecological developments that took place as the nineteenth century progressed. Could it be that other forces were at work while Matthew Arnold was re-introducing William as one of England's preeminent lyric poets?[10] "Home at Grasmere" and the Grasmere journals are in essence incomplete works (and have nothing to do with Arnold's notions of lyric poetry), and yet their publication in the late nineteenth century has encouraged us to find ways to read them as wholes. Kenneth Johnston, for example, uses "Home at Grasmere" as his starting point for his work on *The Recluse*, that incomplete work to end all incomplete works. His brilliant rhetorically oriented reading of the poem, however, leads him to conclude that it "is nothing if not internally coherent, since it virtually implodes itself" (*Wordsworth and* 88). In Johnston's view, a would-be whole crumbles into a heap of fragments because William could never find a satisfactory way of incorporating trouble-filled narratives into his ecstatic vision of Grasmere Vale. Meanwhile, readers of the Grasmere journals have sometimes worked in the opposite direction. That is, they have taken what they perceive to be fragments and made them whole by locating the foundational narratives (and sometimes, as we have seen, the foundational *narrative*) covertly lending them coherence. Both approaches have much to offer while at the same time revealing that a lack of concern for ecology potentially limits our ideas of wholeness. Read from an ecological perspective, however, "Home at Grasmere" and the Grasmere journals look and behave quite a bit differently, the emphasis suddenly falling on their inclusive tendencies. For both works are ultimately processes. And this is only fitting given that they derive their inspiration—take their sustenance—from a particular locale: Grasmere Vale. Dorothy and William undoubtedly felt the pull of place, so much so that they allowed it to shape their practical and creative lives. In fact, if the two of them were engaged in any kind of real project it was to demonstrate the interrelatedness of life and art. In the Grasmere journals this manifests itself as a celebration of daily life, each entry overlapping with the next (and sometimes even with itself, as we see in the entry containing the description of the daffodils) to form an ever-expanding whole. The daffodils are a part of this whole, Dorothy bringing them back home to Grasmere from the banks of Ullswater and giving them new life with the help of her always fecund imagination in the ecosystem of the Grasmere journals themselves.

Chapter Two

The High Road Home: Paths to Ecology in Dorothy Wordsworth's *Recollections of a Tour Made in Scotland*

Implicit in James McKusick's environmental perspective is a distrust of tourism. Proposing that the Romantic period gave us "the first full-fledged ecological writers in the Western literary tradition" (19), McKusick, in his recent study *Green Writing: Romanticism and Ecology*, privileges those writers who demonstrate a thoroughgoing knowledge of place. Perhaps not surprisingly, then, McKusick almost immediately immerses us in the work of William Wordsworth and Samuel Taylor Coleridge, two canonical Romantic poets whose most characteristic work (he argues) grew out of the particular Lake District environment the poets experienced on a daily basis. McKusick subtly underscores this inextricable relationship between poet and environment, however, by first describing the "tradition" that existed before Coleridge and Wordsworth turned their backs on the metropolis of London and sequestered themselves in the north of England. Notice in particular McKusick's careful use of language:

> The tradition of Sensibility, as it developed from Thomson through the poets of the later eighteenth century, falls short of an authentically ecological understanding of the natural world; it reflects an essentially touristic and hierarchical awareness centered on the most spectacular or 'sublime' aspects of nature. . . . The poet is just passing through, on his way to ever more astonishing and delightful scenes; he is not a native inhabitant, and he knows little about the local environment or the everyday activities of the local residents. (23)

In contradistinction to the harried wanderings of these Poets of Feeling, McKusick introduces Wordsworth and Coleridge as exemplars of an emerging ecological tradition, one that effectively supplants the "tradition of Sensibility" through a seemingly conscious rejection of tourism and the touristic:

> Wordsworth and Coleridge are more than just itinerant observers of scenic beauty; they are dwellers in the landscape of the Lake District, and the poetry that they composed in this region often adopts the persona of a speaker whose voice is inflected by the local and personal history of the place he inhabits. Such a perspective may legitimately be termed an ecological view of the natural world, since their poetry consistently expresses a deep and abiding interest in the Earth as a dwelling-place for all living things. (28–29)

Wordsworth and Coleridge's move to the Lake District appears to have coincided with a shift in the meaning of the word "tourist" itself. Refining the *OED*'s account that the originally neutral "tourist" acquires its pejorative sense ("they're obviously *tourists*") "by the middle of the nineteenth century," James Buzard discovers this negative accruement as early as the 1790s. In fact, in order to illustrate his point he refers us specifically to the opening of "The Brothers," which William began composing almost immediately after he and Dorothy had settled in the cottage at Town End at the end of 1799:

> These Tourists, Heaven preserve us! needs must live
> A profitable life: some glance along,
> Rapid and gay, as if the earth were air,
> And they were butterflies to wheel about
> Long as their summer lasted; some, as wise,
> Upon the forehead of a jutting crag
> Sit perch'd with book and pencil on their knee,
> And look and scribble, scribble on and look
> Until a man might travel twelve stout miles,
> Or reap an acre of his neighbour's corn.[1] (1–10)

The "homely" Priest of Ennerdale's amusing protestations seem to accord beautifully with—and indeed provide substance for—McKusick's account of the origins of an ecological tradition of writing. If anything, the poem's abrupt opening (which William apologizes for in a note, explaining that "The Brothers" was to be but one in a series of pastoral poems) dramatically illustrates the dynamics of a new cultural situation. That is to say, the Priest's clearly "inflected" perspective brings "itinerant" tourists into view; it only remains for us to jettison them from a pristine environment, as McKusick implicitly does, in order to perceive the birth of ecological writing in the West.

But appearances can be deceptive. Readers know that the Priest, in spite of his knowledge of the "local and personal history of the place he inhabits," fails to recognize the tourist in question as Leonard, a native inhabitant of Ennerdale who has returned after a long absence to learn the whereabouts—and, as it turns out, fate—of his brother. And I am going to argue that an understanding of an emerging ecological tradition of writing during the Romantic period that does not consider the role tourism and tourists play in its construction is in danger of reenacting the Priest's original misperception. For as it emerges in the literature of the Romantic period, ecology exists in a dialectical relationship with tourism.

In fact, Coleridge and the Wordsworths' move northward was underwritten by tourist practice. We remember that Coleridge was not particularly keen on leaving literary London—that William and Dorothy had to woo him to the north. This courting ritual had occurred as early as December of 1798, while they were all still in Germany, but it seems that they could not be certain of success until after William gave Coleridge a guided tour of the Lake District in October and November of 1799. Stephen Gill succinctly describes the details of the tour and its effect on Coleridge:

> Wordsworth had bombarded him with sensation in a perfectly designed route which led from the domestic and agricultural at Hawkshead and Grasmere to the sublime on Helvellyn to the still more magnificent in Wasdale and Borrowdale before a conclusion of supreme beauty on Ullswater. He had beheld, [Coleridge] said, 'a vision of a fair Country.' (*A Life* 167)

William's calculated maneuverings result in Coleridge's "vision," a process that reflects the curious status of the Lake District at this point in their lives. Of course, very soon they would become dwellers in this magnificent landscape (and for William, Grasmere itself would become his ideal of the "true community" ["Home at Grasmere" 819]). How peculiar, then, that they approach their future home respectively in the guises of tour guide and tourist. Ultimately, however, the Lake District's fragile status as potential home and tourist haven at the end of 1799 represents a dynamic—a merging of knowledge and novelty—that will shape future travel experiences. But of course there will be one significant difference, and that is that all future travel experiences will grow out of—and exist in relation to—firmly held convictions about what it means to be a dweller in a landscape.

"Journals we shall have in number sufficient to fill a Lady's bookshelf,—for all, except my Brother, write a Journal" (*Middle Years, 1812–1820* 625). Dorothy Wordsworth wrote this while touring the Continent in 1820, and it reminds us that all members of the Wordsworth circle (excepting William) at one time or another kept travel journals. Dorothy, however, was the consummate travel writer of her circle, and her *Recollections of a Tour Made in Scotland* is, in the words of Ernest de Selincourt, her "masterpiece" (Dorothy Wordsworth, *Journals* I vii). Begun shortly after returning from their six week tour in September of 1803 but not finished until some twenty months later, the *Recollections* is nevertheless a remarkably coherent work.[2] Indeed, it is more an extended narrative than a journal per se, as Dorothy herself emphasized. "By the bye I am not writing a journal," she explains in a letter to her friend Catherine Clarkson, "for we took no notes, but *recollections* of our Tour in the form of a journal" (*Early Years* 421). Dorothy's careful distinction reveals that her work was not only an act of memory but also a domestic production, and in fact we can—and actually must—trace its origins back to the cottage at Town End itself. In my previous chapter on the Grasmere journals, I designate Dove Cottage as a kind of centre from which Dorothy worked, her seemingly amorphous descriptions accreting to form the ecosystem of the journals themselves. Only eight months separate the final—and, perhaps significantly, incomplete—entry of the Grasmere journals and the beginning of the *Recollections*. And while we might perceive a kind of sea change having taken place as Dorothy approaches the writing of a travel narrative (the amorphousness of the Grasmere journals becoming the coherence of the *Recollections*), we also discover the works' deep similarities—as long, that is, as we do not lose sight of the ecological centre from which Dorothy worked.

For her imagination was centripetally oriented, shaping and revolving itself around a clear idea of home.[3] As early as 1793 Dorothy envisioned for her friend Jane Pollard a scene of domestic tranquility, one so snugly conceived that as it progresses its fragile relationship to a natural environment (established through Dorothy's reference to the seasons) appears to recede, leaving us with a lingering sense of a thoroughly sequestered domesticity:

> I look forward with full confidence to the Happiness of receiving you in my little Parsonage, I hope you will spend at least a year with me. I have laid the particular scheme of happiness for each Season. When I think of Winter I hasten to furnish our little Parlour, I close the Shutters, set out the Tea-table, brighten the Fire. When our Refreshment is ended I produce our Work, and William brings his book to our Table and contributes at once to our Instruction and amusement, and at Intervals we

lay aside the Book and each hazard our observations upon what has been read without fear of Ridicule or Censure. We talk over past days, we do not sigh for any Pleasures beyond our humble Habitation "The central point of all our joys." (*Early Years* 87–88)

The symbolic act here would appear to be Dorothy's closing of the shutters. She shuts nature out (although admittedly she envisions a winter scene), emphasizing from that point on human interaction, especially as it relates to those particularly human artifacts—books. In fact, Dorothy's early fantasy, for it is just that, seems to contradict William's advice, apparently addressed to Hazlitt, of only five years later:

> Books! 'tis a dull and endless strife,
> Come, hear the woodland linnet,
> How sweet his music; on my life
> There's more of wisdom in it. (9–12)

McKusick concentrates in particular on "The Tables Turned" (from which the above stanza comes) and "Expostulation and Reply" in his environmental reading of William's poetry, stating of the former that it "turns the tables upon the entire Western tradition of scientific knowledge . . . [proposing] a new role for humankind among the speaking presences of the natural world" (60). Of course, William would work his environmental magic on Dorothy herself in "Lines Written at a Small Distance from my House," and we can easily imagine her at that later date (1798) putting on her "woodland dress, / And bring[ing] no book" (38–39) as she goes outside in the fresh spring air to join her brother. But in 1793 it would seem that Dorothy had not yet learned the significance of living in a state of "wise passiveness" ("Expostulation and Reply" 24). Instead, she brightens the fire in their parlour, desiring no "Pleasures beyond [their] humble Habitation."

But the full description reads "we do not sigh for any Pleasures beyond our humble Habitation '*The central point of all our joys*'" (my emphasis). And that last phrase, which Dorothy borrows from William's *Descriptive Sketches* (1793), offers us a glimpse of what we might describe as Dorothy's intuitive ecological sense. For William's centripetal language uncannily looks forward to "Home at Grasmere," (or rather, it does after Dorothy incorporates it into her description) his most thoroughly ecological poem. We recall that in that work, the bulk of which William composed in 1800, just after Dorothy's fantasy of a "humble Habitation" had become a reality, he describes Grasmere itself as "A termination, and a last retreat, / A Centre, come from wheresoe'er you will. . . ." (166–67). To be sure, in 1793 Dorothy could not have foreseen either that they would eventually live in Grasmere or that William would celebrate their homecoming in perhaps some of the most passionate verse he was ever to write. Moreover, my object is not to gaze in crystal balls; rather, I wish to underscore the radical consistency of William and Dorothy's vision, a vision that negotiates what we have come to understand as the ecological in relation to a deeply felt domesticity.

And nowhere is this more apparent than in the *Recollections*, a work that would seem to challenge Dorothy's domestic ecology simply for being a travel narrative but which paradoxically illustrates how firmly entrenched her unique environmental perspective actually was. I have already taken note of the work's remarkable coherence, and what follows will not contradict Carol Kyros Walker's findings. At the same time, though, an ecological reading of perhaps Dorothy's most satisfying travel narrative locates an order rather different from those readings that define the work in more rigidly generic terms. For example, John Glendening contextualizes the *Recollections* not only in relation to travel writing in the eighteenth century as a developing practice but more specifically in relation to the cultural construction of a "wild" Scotland that grew out of that development. The result is a detailed mapping of a fascinating historical and cultural phenomenon; however, in summarizing his interpretation of the *Recollections* he shows a curious need to contain Dorothy's method. "[Her] tourism," he writes, "is conventional in its professed dismissal of conventional tourism, in its tacit acceptance of the picturesque, in its related avoidance of pictorial and cultural ugliness, and in its desire to communicate and retain the touristic experience. . . ." (135). Dorothy's work offers more than enough evidence to substantiate these claims, as Glendening's meticulous interpretation demonstrates. But that plethora of evidence might, in fact, ultimately threaten Glendening's reading, for as Onno Oerlemans has pointed out in his recent ecocritical study, *Romanticism and the Materiality of Nature*, "[m]ost travel writing is by its very nature uneconomical, recording an excess of fact, whose significance is clear to neither the writer nor the reader" (178–79). It would seem that Glendening's ideologically oriented reading depends upon an understanding of tourism as a culturally "scripted," ultimately homogenous experience. Applied specifically to the *Recollections*, however, Oerlemans' observation (which actually just precedes his consideration of Dorothy's journal) suggests quite the opposite. That is to say, Dorothy's travel narrative embraces multitudes: it shapes itself to Glendening's analysis but will not be reduced, and in fact in its very adaptability behaves surprisingly like an ecosystem.[4] For the *Recollections* gives us not just tourism, but *tourisms*, which is perhaps more a reflection on the tourist in question than anything else.

Of course, Dorothy was a devotee of the picturesque, taking its principles with her on her travels. According to John Nabholtz, when she was "examining the natural scene, she was looking for harmonious visual compositions which brought into unity varied and intricate parts—in effect, the definition of pictorial composition developed in the picturesque literature of the eighteenth century" (120). Nabholtz's seminal essay, "Dorothy Wordsworth and the Picturesque," focuses in particular on the *Recollections*. And once we have absorbed its illustration of the conventions shaping Dorothy's perception of nature we detect the picturesque in the *Recollections* at almost every turn. (We also perceive an important foundation for Glendening's culturally oriented interpretation). It certainly plays a role in her famous description of the Highland boy, whose "appearance was in the highest degree moving to . . . [her] imagination" (286). It also, however, crops up in less sublime situations, such as when, making their way to the Trossachs, and hoping to hire a boat so that they can go out on Loch Katrine, Dorothy enters a "traditional" Highland dwelling for the first time:

> We found the ferryman at work in the field above his hut, and he was at liberty to go with us, but, being wet and hungry, we begged that he would let us sit by his fire till we had refreshed ourselves. This was the first genuine Highland hut we had been in. We entered by the cowhouse, the house-door being within, at right angles to the outer door. The woman was distressed that she had a bad fire, but she heaped up some dry peats and heather, and, blowing it with her breath, in a short time raised a blaze that scorched us into comfortable feelings. A small part of the smoke found its way out of the hole in the chimney, the rest through the open window-panes, one of which was within the recess of the fireplace, and made a frame to a little picture of the restless lake and the opposite shore, seen when the outer door was open. (270)

Dorothy's imaginative reconstruction evokes the hut's spatial qualities, subtly transforming it into a comfortable domestic viewing-station in the process. For once they have been "scorched . . . into comfortable feelings," she perceives the scene from a kind of wry distance, watching the smoke make its leisurely—and for Dorothy typically Scottish—way out of the hut. The scene ends with Dorothy's picturesquely trained eye falling on the natural frame of the window itself, her description of "the restless lake and the opposite shore" making a piquant contrast to the cozy—if also somewhat smoky—stillness of her surroundings. In Nabholtz's terms, she forges "varied and intricate parts" into a new picturesque unity for her (English) readers.

If we define Dorothy exclusively as a picturesque tourist, we might say that she hearkens back to James McKusick's notion of a "tradition of Sensibility." She "is just passing through, on [her] way to ever more astonishing and delightful scenes" (23). Of course, Dorothy herself would never have denied that she went to Scotland in search of novelty, and in fact in the midst of her description of their journey through the region of Loch Lomond (the chosen destination of every tourist of Scotland in the eighteenth century) exclaims, "[w]herever we looked, it was a delightful feeling that there was something beyond" (253). From McKusick's point of view, Dorothy must always exist "beyond" the landscape she moves through. Indeed, her frequently quoted claim that "Scotland is the country above all others that I have seen, in which a man of imagination may carve out his own pleasures" (214) suggests the intense role fantasy plays in the tourist experience. Far from being a genuine work of ecology, then, Dorothy's travel narrative evokes through the use of memory a landscape that only existed as an imaginative experience in the first place. Dorothy is twice removed from her environment.

Or is she? Since writing is an inherently rational activity, we might say that any relationship with a natural environment articulated through the medium of the written word involves an act of the imagination. Are the Grasmere journals and the *Recollections* so very different then? "The moonshine like herrings in the water" (30). We will certainly not find anything in the *Recollections* approximating the rare immanence of this description. Indeed, the vantage point from which Dorothy describes the scene at least in part seems responsible for its shimmering luminosity. For in the act of writing she so wholly engages with her surroundings that she appears to lose herself entirely within them, "[a]mong the woods and copses" ("Tintern Abbey" 13).

Or in the act of writing is she simply removed from them? Here, we might wish to take note of McKusick's sensibly stringent definition of the writer as environmentalist. "Just as all politics is local," he writes, "so too all ecology is local; and a true ecological writer must be 'rooted' in the landscape, instinctively attuned to the changes of the Earth and its inhabitants" (24). Dorothy's ability to describe landscape so purely in the Grasmere journals reflects the degree to which she is "rooted" within the Grasmere environment. And yet, I would argue that the ecologically oriented reader tends to accept on faith that daily interaction with a known landscape necessarily affects the writing experience itself—that that writing experience is more genuine because of its (supposedly) firm empirical foundations. Rather than attack the philosophical roots (and branches) of environmental writing, however, I simply wish to point out that on some level the ecological writer always engages imaginatively with her or his surroundings. Indeed, Dorothy's famous description of the moonshine is itself a trope-driven, miniature *tour de force*. As a result, we need not reject the *Recollections* as a genuinely ecological work because of its purported abstract methodology—that is, because she began writing the journal only after the tour, using no notes. Moreover, the fact that Dorothy composes her travel journal from the vantage point of the "*oikos*" (root word of "ecology" meaning "home" or "dwelling place") affects its very subject matter, since Dorothy's domestic perspective (the ground from which she always worked) remains firmly intact in the *Recollections*. We might say, then, that Romantic ecological writing is an inherently interrelated activity involving a classic fusion of mind and matter.[5]

Because Dorothy composed her journal after their tour, she tends toward a synthetic view of experience, which is to say that she frequently pauses to summarize events and express the lasting effect they have had on her. One such moment occurs at a crucial point in the narrative, although Dorothy's approach to composition is so charmingly casual that we might read right past it. Dorothy, William, and Coleridge have covered much ground since entering the Highlands at Luss (which as a good tourist Dorothy knows represents "the place where . . . that country begins" [247]), and they have come across several curiosities along the way, including the Highland hut. Interestingly, however, Dorothy's summary of what was in effect the first stage of their journey through the Highlands at the beginning of their third week of travel organizes itself around her memory of two Highland girls. William later commemorated the encounter in "To a Highland Girl," creatively conflating the two girls into a composite figure in the process, and in fact Dorothy's musings immediately precede her incorporation of the poem into her narrative.

> The hospitality we had met with at the two cottages and Mr. Macfarlane's gave us very favourable impressions on this our first entrance into the Highlands, and at this day the innocent merriment of the girls, with their kindness to us, and the beautiful figure and face of the elder, come to my mind whenever I think of the ferry-house and waterfall at Loch Lomond, and I never think of the two girls but the whole image of that romantic spot is before me, a living image, as it will be to my dying day. (283)

The "innocent merriment of the girls" unites with Dorothy's memory of "the ferry-house and waterfall at Loch Lomond" to form a "living image," which results in mild hyperbole as Dorothy vows to recall the intricate portrait to her "dying day." In effect, what we have here is an example of the picturesque writ large, a synthesis involving not just a particular scene but an interrelated collection of scenes all sharing a Highland setting.

That quietly arresting—and nearly Coleridgean—phrase "living image," however, compels us to move beyond picturesque landscapes into Romantic environments—that is, if we wish to read Dorothy as thoroughly as we can. Of course, the phrase is absolutely accurate (and for Dorothy accuracy was everything) in that it refers specifically to the Highland girls; they are the catalyst for her recollections, as opposed to, say, a well-known feature of the Highland landscape. The image is, strictly speaking, living. It is also, however, remarkably compressed—so jewel-like in its construction and finish that it might blind us to Dorothy's organizing energies, which manifest themselves in subtly surprising ways here. For Dorothy works inclusively, organizing her description initially around the two Highland girls, almost perceiving them as ontologically separate from their surroundings. But the pleasant intrusion of the ferry-house and waterfall at Loch Lomond into Dorothy's recollection of the scene suggests a more firmly rooted ontology. Simplifying the process (that is, understanding her essentially holistic approach in more linear terms), we might say that Dorothy temporarily removes the Highland girls from their surroundings before imaginatively re-perceiving them in relation to—and ultimately understanding them as a part of—their environment. Her ontology, paradoxically linked to a clearly established picturesque tradition, blooms into an ecology.

I mentioned earlier that Dorothy's recollection of the Highland girls occurs at a crucial point in the narrative, and that is because the encounter itself occurred at a crucial point during the tour. Oerlemans makes an interesting observation about the tendency of travel writing to take on the shape of tours themselves:

> In general, travel writing avoids extended expectations of narrative except in terms of the route of the voyage, which rarely has anything like a climax or an expectation of closure—the trip ends when time or money runs out, when the circuit of the journey has been made, and so on; return trips are generally given scant attention. (162)

Even a cursory glance at the *Recollections* will reveal that its narrative follows the route of the tour itself, which roughly speaking traces a large circle from west to east (represented by the cities of Glasgow and Edinburgh respectively) in a north to south direction. The journal opens with Dorothy, William, and Coleridge leaving Keswick and closes with Dorothy and William returning to the cottage at Town End (Coleridge having parted with them after only two weeks into what wound up being a six-week tour). It certainly does not have anything resembling a narrative climax. And yet, their journey into the Highlands, which forms the centre of the circle of the tour, represents a slight departure from one aspect of Oerleman's paradigm, for once they enter that most celebrated of regions the trio embarks on a series of miniature "return trips." And eventually, Dorothy and William spontaneously decide to re-trace, only in backwards fashion, their journey through the Trossachs. It might seem a small point, but this desire to revisit Highland landscapes in the midst of the tour itself suggests their need to disrupt the predictable linearity of the travel experience itself.

From Glendening's perspective, Dorothy and William's return trips might simply illustrate their "professed dismissal of conventional tourism" (135). In fact, they do not consider themselves tourists at all and are thus constantly looking for ways to move off the beaten track. Far from being spontaneous, or "natural," then, Dorothy and William's decision to revisit the Trossachs (the touristic heart of the Scottish Highlands) might be another example of scripted tourist behaviour. The ideological signs point us in such an interpretive direction.

We have, however, been following Dorothy down an ecological path—an alternate route worth pursuing in part, I think, because it affords us access to the unconventional aspects of her tourist practice. And given Dorothy's passionate recollection of the Highland girls, as well as her description of the first Highland hut she entered, we should not be surprised to find ourselves substituting either "female" or "feminine" for "unconventional." Susan Levin's insights into Dorothy's observational tendencies while travelling further secures our place on the High Road of ecology:

> [S]he tends to focus on the women she encounters in her travels more than on the men. The access she, as a woman, has to other women and the part she gives these contacts to play in her travel journals individualize her work. Her descriptions of women help characterize the country she wishes to describe at the same time as they help define her own being as a woman and a writer. (81)

Levin uncovers the multifariousness of Dorothy's interest in her own kind; she also (without intending it, which perhaps makes her insights all the more compelling) clarifies her ecological perspective, giving it a distinctly feminine slant. For we have already seen how the Highland girls "help characterize the country [Dorothy] wishes to describe." Indeed, I would argue that Dorothy's sense of the One Life (to borrow Coleridge's famous phrase—and which has an ecological significance of its own[6]) as we receive it in her description of the Highland girls ultimately defines "her own being as a woman and a writer."

Not everyone would be willing to concede this, however—at least not when considering her travel writing. And perhaps now is a good time to consider one of the more problematic aspects of Dorothy's stance as a tourist. Rachel Mayer Brownstein puts her finger on the problem and in the process compartmentalizes Dorothy according to commonly held opinions about her work:

> The Journals she wrote on the Continent—including the *Journal of Visit to Hamburgh, etc.* of 1798—and in Scotland reveal a maiden English traveler, suspicious, scared, nosy, and homesick. She clucks about dirt and manners and the size of rooms and the lack of bells and the price of food and its quality. . . . She is more to our taste when she excitedly glimpses a freer, less tidy, and less tangible world. . . ." (60)

We find precisely such a world reflected in Dorothy's beautiful description of the moonshine, although an ecologically-minded reader might have misgivings about that phrase "less tangible." For it seems to me that in the Grasmere journals Dorothy fuses different elements of a tangibly intangible world (made up of "rocks and stones and trees"—and human beings) into a new, extraordinary whole, exactly as we have seen her do in the *Recollections* in relation to the Highland girls as a matter of fact. Nevertheless, Brownstein's assessment partially explains why, as Hunter Davies points out, the Grasmere journals have "usually been the best-selling book every year at the Dove Cottage bookshop" (133).

Brownstein's view, then, is a popular one. It is also absolutely accurate, as the following example from the *Recollections* will illustrate.

> The New Inn [in Lanerk] is a handsome old stone building, formerly a gentleman's house. We were conducted into a palour, where people had been drinking; the tables were unwiped, chairs in disorder, the floor dirty, and the smell of liquors was most offensive. We were tired, however, and rejoiced in our tea. (219)

We find such descriptions again and again in Dorothy's travel journals. Whether she is in Lanerk on the road to Glasgow and eventually the Highlands, or in the Highlands themselves, Dorothy has high (English) standards and constantly sizes up what she finds while travelling according to them. This is connected to another aspect of Dorothy's tourism: her tendency to perceive Scotland—and the Highlands in particular—through a Grasmere lens. John Nabholtz understands this tendency in relation to the picturesque, and in so doing re-focuses our attention on Grasmere as the "Centre"—the "Unity entire"—from which Dorothy works.

> . . . Dorothy's visual sense had not been perfectly satisfied during her tour of Scotland; she continually missed the landscapes of the Lake Country, with their more consistent and characteristic picturesque quality. And she maintained the same aesthetic point of view throughout the rest of her life, whether she was observing scenery in other parts of England or on the continent. (126)

Taken together, Brownstein and Nabholtz's observations suggest Dorothy's provincialism. At worst, she was something of a picturesque tourist snob (although this is emphatically not Nabholtz's perspective); at best, she simply felt more at home in Grasmere. In the end, however, neither extreme satisfactorily describes Dorothy's tourist stance, and that is because such divisive categories work against a fundamental concept of ecology. For the Grasmere journals and the *Recollections* are interrelated works, even though this might not appear to be the case at first, or even second, glance. Reading ecologically, however, compels us to shift our "aesthetic point of view," the result being that we perceive beyond apparent contrarieties into the deeper harmonies sustaining Dorothy's ecological vision.

As a way into this vision (and we shall soon see the appropriateness of such language), let us reconsider the Highland hut that so captivated Dorothy's imagination. I have already mentioned the role return visits play in Dorothy and William's tourism, and here (on the same day—August 27th) we find Dorothy returning to the hut after a long day's excursion up and down Loch Katrine, the description of which also forms an integral part of the long entry. "It was dark when we landed, and on entering the house I was sick with cold," she remembers (276). After changing out of their wet clothes, however, they enjoy a "pan of coffee" Coleridge had prepared for them, "thankful for a shelter" (276). Eventually, Dorothy goes to bed, but she is simply too stimulated to sleep. Recounting the scene from the cottage

at Town End, she recaptures the domestic wonders of that evening spent in
the Highlands:

> I went to bed some time before the family. The door was shut between
> us, and they had a bright fire, which I could not see; but the light it sent
> up among the varnished rafters and beams, which crossed each other
> in almost as intricate and fantastic a manner as I have seen the under-
> boughs of a large beech-tree withered by the depth of the shade above,
> produced the most beautiful effect that can be conceived. It was like what
> I should suppose an underground cave or temple to be, with a dripping
> or moist roof, and the moonlight entering in upon it by some means
> or other, and yet the colours were more like melted gems. . . . [T]he
> unusualness of my situation prevented me from sleeping. I could hear
> the waves beat against the shore of the lake; a little 'syke' close to the
> door made a much louder noise; and when I sate up in my bed I could
> see the lake through an open window-place at the bed's head. Add to
> this, it rained all night. I was less occupied by remembrance of the Tros-
> sachs, beautiful as they were, than the vision of the Highland hut, which
> I could not get out of my head. I thought of the Fairyland of Spenser,
> and what I had read in romance at other times, and then, what a feast
> would it be for a London pantomime-maker, could he but transplant it
> to Drury Lane, with all its beautiful colours! (277–78)

It would be perfectly reasonable for an ecologically-minded reader to overlook
this fantastic passage and read back into the long entry for a more suitable
example of Dorothy's ecological perspective. One might want to concentrate,
for example, on her account of their excursion to and on Loch Katrine, ques-
tioning in the process to what extent she eschews picturesque categories. But
this, I think, would be to overlook Dorothy's awareness of domestic environments, an awareness that informs her ecological perspective from the very
beginning—as soon as she expresses her desire for a genuine home.

At bottom, Dorothy's description of her imaginative wanderings deep
in the heart of the Highland hut is a *tour de force* of feminine writing. And
it takes its place beside a series of descriptions (perhaps the most brightly
coloured threads in the fabric of the journal) which find Dorothy exploring
the borders of feminine imagery. And yet, while several critics have examined
this aspect of the journal, even in relation to this passage in particular, they
have inexplicably overlooked, or at least taken for granted, Grasmere's presence in the scene.[7] To be sure, the scene's conclusion, with its stylized evocation of an urban environment (itself inspired by a literary environment—the

"Fairyland of Spenser"), strongly suggests the virtual disappearance of Grasmere from Dorothy's imaginative horizon. Entering the Highland hut, Dorothy is soon on the High Road to London. We remember, however, that Dorothy works from Grasmere, which means that during the writing moment she engages in a kind of environmental balancing act. For example, she had obviously never been in either "an underground cave or temple," but she had observed her fair share of trees—and in fact several spring up beautifully and memorably in her Grasmere journals.[8] We can even imagine Dorothy taking a break from the heat of composing this scene to look out one of the windows of the cottage at Town End. She rests her eyes on a favourite birch (not beech) tree, her imagination poised—like one of her cherished swallows—to take flight once again.

"I was less occupied by remembrance of the Trossachs, beautiful as they were, than the vision of the Highland hut, which I could not get out of my head." Dorothy's highly imaginative description builds effortlessly to this climax, but that doesn't make it any less audacious. We have already witnessed the transformation of this space into a kind of homely—but also sophisticated—viewing-station. With the onset of evening, however, Dorothy turns to her interior surroundings and discovers a domestic landscape that rivals—and even supplants—the celebrated Trossachs themselves. Such an interiorization of picturesque principles is absolutely in keeping with Dorothy's quietly subversive aesthetic; it is also, however, a vital aspect of her ecological sense. For ultimately (picturesque) tourism and ecology are interrelated aspects of a larger process of modernization—a process that manifests itself in Dorothy's life and work as an endless quest for home.

We do not naturally think of Dorothy in perpetual pursuit of a home. After all, we associate her with the Grasmere journals, which is simply to say that we associate her with a particular place—and rightfully so. Nevertheless, it is important to remember that at crucial times in her life the idea of a home was just that—an idea, as we have already seen in the vision of home she describes in 1793 for her friend Jane Pollard. Let us, however, move forward just a little in time (while still remaining outside Grasmere itself) to 1795—that is, to that time when the idea of home was about to be replaced by the thing itself. She again writes to her friend Jane (Marshall—she has since married).

> I am going now to tell you what is for your own eyes and ears alone. I need say no more than this I am sure, to insure your most careful secrecy. Know then that I am going to live in Dorsetshire. Let me, however, methodically state the whole plan, and then my dearest Jane

> I doubt not you will rejoice in the prospect which at last opens before
> me of having, at least for a time a comfortable home, in a house of my
> own. You know the pleasure which I have always attached to the idea of
> home, a blessing which I so early lost. . . . (*Early Years* 146)

Barely contained excitement leads to more sober reflection as Dorothy out-
lines for her friend the details of an approaching boon borne out of loss—the
loss we know shaped her idea of having a home in the first place. And it is
precisely here, I think, that we discover Dorothy's emerging modern consciousness. For in announcing her intention to become a dweller in a particular landscape (and in the process laying the foundations for the Alfoxden
journal, perhaps her first fully realized ecological work[9]), she also acknowledges the fragility of their plan. She hopes "at least for a time" to have a "comfortable home." Dorothy's early experiences have taught her not to count
on having a permanent home, and yet instinctively this is what she desires
the most. This means that for Dorothy the very idea of possessing a home
is fraught with anxiety, no matter how well she disguises it. Fortuitously,
however (but also perhaps inevitably, given that her condition is a reflection
of historical processes), the emergence of tourism in the eighteenth-century
gives Dorothy the means of transforming latent anxiety into sheer delight.

And this perhaps accounts for the kind of tourist she was. For in following Dorothy through Scotland, we cannot help but notice how easily and
naturally she gravitates towards domestic environments (to the point of for-
getting the Trossachs themselves!). In fact, this tendency is so prevalent that
I believe we should think of her as an environmental tourist. But what precisely does this mean?

In *The Song of the Earth*, Jonathan Bate speculates on the origins of
the word "environment." He points out that we will not find it in Johnson's
dictionary and also suggests that the word would have been "barely available"
to a writer such as Jane Austen, which in turn means that it would have been
barely available to Dorothy. He muses further on the matter.

> I suspect that the word "environment" began to be applied to social
> contexts . . . because of the feeling of the alienation of city-dwelling
> which was identified by Wordsworth and others. That is to say, prior
> to the nineteenth century there was no need for a word to describe the
> influence of physical conditions on persons and communities because it
> was self-evident that personal and communal identity were intimately
> related to physical setting. The influence of, for instance, the climate
> and the soil was taken for granted. But from the late eighteenth century

onwards, there was an increasing awareness of industry's tendency to alter the quality of our surroundings, even to affect the air we breathe. (13–14)

I have already suggested that Dorothy's deep desire for a home (the *oikos*) is the result of an earlier loss. Bate's insights, however, allow us to place this dynamic in a larger framework. Of course, Dorothy never experienced the alienation of the city-dweller (although in this context it is interesting to note her general abhorrence of urban environments[10]). Nevertheless, she had been uprooted from a cherished place—a place she was able to perceive as an environment only after she was forced to leave. And it seems to me that we can understand Dorothy's marvelous eye for detail in light of this life-shaping moment. That is to say, Dorothy's need to write her surroundings suggests her desire to heal a gap she experienced very early in life. At the same time, though, it is precisely this dynamic that made her a model tourist and consummate travel writer. Tourism is a quintessentially modern phenomenon, and ceaseless motion is its *raison d'être*. Dorothy eagerly took part in this phenomenon—we remember that she exulted in the "delightful feeling that there was [always] something beyond" (253). And yet, she recollects the tour while home at Grasmere. She seeks comfort in the *oikos* while musing on the ceaseless motion she so recently experienced and which is perhaps the defining feature of the modern world she was born into.

When Dorothy wrote of her delightfully sleepless night spent in the Highland hut, she did so "for the sake of Friends who could not [be] with [them] at the time" (*Letters . . . Early Years* 598). As we have seen, however, the vantage point from which she worked engaged her in a subtly more complicated process. Rooted back in the Grasmere landscape, Dorothy imaginatively re-enters a clearly defined domestic space—an ordinary enough activity (particularly since she had been envisioning domestic environments for well over a decade), but one that results in a rather extraordinary vision. Of course, Dorothy would never have referred to her recollection of the Highland hut as an ecological vision, but given our understanding of the development of environmental awareness in the nineteenth century I believe we should. Ecology envisions wholeness; it perceives the interrelationship of all organic and inorganic matter in what we have come to call an ecosystem. Like tourism, however, ecology emerges as a result of—and in the case of ecology itself also as a challenge to—the forces of modernity. It seeks to make whole what humankind increasingly threatens to destroy. Thus, when Dorothy enters the Highland hut she does so as a tourist and prototypical ecologist. Her natural delight in domestic environments allows her to perceive that "personal and communal identity" exist within the "physical setting" of the hut itself. As a tourist, however, she also understands that her experience of this uniquely Scottish environment is fleeting—that ultimately she must recall it as a vision. Interestingly, Dorothy's diction mirrors Coleridge's, for we remember his breathless description of the Lake District (an environment he came to as a tourist—and eventually returned to as a dweller). He had beheld, he said, "a vision of a fair Country." Perhaps fittingly, Dorothy was the recipient of this vision, for the phrase appears in the letter he sent back to the Hutchinson farm, which was where Dorothy was staying at the time of William and Coleridge's tour.[11] It seems, then, that for both Dorothy and Coleridge visions of wholeness occur while on the High Road home.

Chapter Three

The Illuminated Earth:
Dorothy Wordsworth's Ecopoetry

"What I came to say was,
teach the children about the cycles.
The life cycles. All the other cycles.
That's what it's all about about, and it's all forgot."
Gary Snyder, "For/From Lew"[1]

Readers of Dorothy Wordsworth are familiar with her failed attempt to compose poetry on the night of March 18, 1802. "The moon retired again & appeared & disappeared several times before I reached home," she writes in her Grasmere journals:

> Once there was no moonlight to be seen but upon the Island house & the promontory of the Island where it stands. 'That needs must be a holy place' &c—&c. I had many exquisite feelings when I saw this lowly Building in the waters among the dark & lofty hills, with that bright soft light upon it—it made me more than half a poet. I was tired when I reached home I could not sit down to reading & tried to write verses but alas! I gave up expecting William & went soon to bed. (81)

Of course, we know that by 1815 William began what became a habit of including a few of Dorothy's poems in his collections, and Susan Levin's work now allows us to estimate that she in fact composed as many as twenty-five during the course of her lifetime.[2] To be sure, this is not the richest of poetic harvests, even when considering that severe physical and mental illness nearly silenced her for the last twenty-five years of her life. Nevertheless, we now have proof that this "half a poet" at times kindled and wrote complete poems.

But where did they come from? Under what conditions did Dorothy successfully compose poetry? Interestingly, we need not look farther than the previous entry of the Grasmere journals to discover poetry in the making. It's just that we have not traditionally attributed its three lines of verse to Dorothy herself.

Like so many other days in the spring of 1802 (the season that inaugurated what we now think of as the "great creative year"), Wednesday, March 17th was devoted to poetry:

> William went up into the Orchard and finished the Poem [presumably "The Emigrant Mother"[3]]. Mrs Luff & Mrs Ollif called I went with Mrs O to the top of the White Moss—Mr O met us & I went to their house he offered me manure for the garden. I went & sate with W & walked backwards and forwards in the Orchard till dinner time—he read me his poem. (79)

Dorothy's Grasmere journals are especially valuable for their illumination of William's creative process, so what could be more natural than to continue reading this entry with Dorothy's interests in mind, namely her brother and his daily poetic endeavours? The entry I have just quoted from continues as follows:

> I broiled Beefsteaks. After dinner we made a pillow of my shoulder, I read to him & my Beloved slept—I afterwards got him the pillows & he was lying with his head on the table when Miss Simpson came in. She stayed tea. I went with her to Rydale. No letters! A sweet Evening as it had been a sweet day, a grey evening, & I walked quietly along the side of Rydale Lake with quiet thoughts—the hills & the Lake were still—the Owls had not begun to hoot, & the little Birds had given over singing. I looked before me & I saw a red light upon Silver How as if coming out of the vale below
>
> 'There was a light of most strange birth
> A Light that came out of the earth
> And spread along the dark hill-side.'
>
> Thus I was going on when I saw the shape of my Beloved in the Road at a little distance—we turned back to see the light but it was fading—almost gone. (79–80)

In her 1958 edition of the Grasmere journals, Helen Darbishire conjectures that Dorothy here quotes (but it seems would have originally recited) lost lines from *Peter Bell*, a claim we might feel inclined to accept without further thought, even if we do not consider ourselves prosodists.[4] For on this day, Dorothy fully immersed herself in William's compositional efforts. She walked "backwards and forwards" with him while he worked (albeit on another poem), so it makes sense that his poetry in general would have been very much with her that day, finding its proper release as she later indulged in a solitary evening walk. But if this is true, why does Pamela Woof entertain the idea that Dorothy herself might have composed these lines? Woof does not support her claim with hard evidence[5]; she simply tantalizes us with the possibility—perhaps because she knows that this might be enough to tease us into a consideration of our own reading biases.

The simple truth is that neither Woof nor I can prove conclusively that Dorothy wrote the three lines of verse in question. Fortunately, however, my consideration of Dorothy's poetry does not hinge on such proof. Instead, I would like to offer Dorothy's journal entry for March 17, 1802 as an example of her environmental approach to poetry—an approach that emerges when we imaginatively participate in Dorothy's daily life, the stuff of virtually all her writing, including her poetry.

And an important aspect of this imaginative participation is our willing suspension of disbelief. That is, we should be willing to entertain the possibility that Dorothy engaged in original poetic composition on this particular day. Darbishire's suggestion that Dorothy in fact quotes William's verses implicitly involves both reader and writer in abstract processes, which is to say that we perhaps too coolly observe Dorothy imposing pre-existing language on to an experience in order to make sense of it. If these verses are Dorothy's, however, it means that they are the result of her (solitary, we notice) walking experience, and this in turn puts us in a position to read more holistically, and thus more accurately. For as James McKusick has recently illustrated, the Romantic poets (including Dorothy, I will argue, although McKusick does not discuss her work) were instrumental "in creating a new, holistic way of perceiving the natural world" (11). Dorothy's journal entry beautifully captures this new, holistic perspective as a process, offering us a glimpse of not just a poet but an ecopoet at work.

"Reverie, solitude, walking: to turn these experiences into language is to be an ecopoet." Jonathan Bate's definition illuminates Dorothy's activities on March 17, 1802. Or is it the other way around? Bate reaches his conclusions through an examination of Rousseau, but they apply to Dorothy's daily life as well. Consider his very next sentence: "Ecopoetry is not a description of dwelling with the earth, not a disengaged thinking about it, but an experiencing of it" (*Song* 42). Dorothy takes her solitary way through a landscape she has come to know intimately since her arrival in Grasmere at the end of 1799, and it results in a spontaneous overflow of poetry that presumably would have continued had William not interrupted her reverie. For she points out that she was "going on" (that is, creating poetry) when she saw "the shape of [her] Beloved in the Road." Here, we could consider more closely the many challenges Dorothy faced as a poet—for example, the fact that she shared her life with a brother who was working hard to rival, if not actually surpass, the achievements of Shakespeare and Milton. (In this context, Dorothy's description of her brother's indistinct shape suddenly appearing on the scene might acquire a symbolic significance. He emerges as a kind of beguiling force, distracting her from her creative activities.) In fact, their complicated relationship has formed the basis for some especially penetrating analyses of her poetry.[6] And yet, this journal entry also reminds us that Dorothy's creative efforts, no matter how fleeting or unsatisfactory they may at times seem to us, take place in Grasmere, a clearly defined environment that ultimately subsumes—but which also nourishes and sustains—even Dorothy and William's relationship.

The Grasmere journals, then, offer a glimpse of an ecopoet in the making, while I would argue that the poems Dorothy eventually went on to complete are the fruits of her ecological maturation. Of course, it might be lamentable that this development went unrecorded and that nearly three years separate the sudden cessation of her journals (for recall that they end in mid-sentence) and the completion of her first extant poem.[7] Nevertheless, the ecologically oriented reader is now poised to perceive the process as captured in her journal entry in the poems themselves through an understanding of them as miniature ecosystems—textual extensions of the Grasmere environment Dorothy knew and loved so well.

Three of Dorothy's poems, "An address to a Child in a high wind," "Grasmere—A Fragment," and "Floating Island at Hawkshead," have much in common from an ecological point of view, and yet their distinct differences (substantive as well as tonal) afford us a concentrated glimpse of the poet's range. Dorothy appears to have composed "An address to a Child in a high wind" some time in 1806, making it one of her earliest poems. It is also one of the closest poetic links we have to the Grasmere journals, since its speaker explores her environment from the vantage point of the cottage at Town End. In fact, exactly halfway through the poem we will find ourselves inside Dove Cottage itself, where we will discover we have perhaps been all along. Initially, however, the speaker (whom I will from now on refer to simply as Dorothy) concentrates solely on the wind, playfully describing it for the benefit and solace of her youthful charge.

What way does the wind come? what way does he go?
He rides over the water and over the snow,
Through the valley, and over the hill
And roars as loud as a thundering Mill.
He tosses about in every bare tree,
As, if you look up you may plainly see
But how he will come, and whither he goes
There's never a Scholar in England knows. (1–8)

We have long associated Romantic poetry with aeolian visitations, but Dorothy's poem offers an alternative to the archetypal model outlined by M. H. Abrams.[8] For instead of apostrophizing the wind (thus adopting the kind of self-reflexive stance we find in the famous opening lines of *The Prelude*), Dorothy addresses a child, an invocation utterly consistent with everything we know about her. Clearly a children's poem, "An address" remains consistently childlike without ever becoming childish (that first stanza sets the tone), perhaps because its subject is one of the most mysterious forces of nature—a force that ultimately eludes the grasp of both adult and child.

As the first stanza also demonstrates, however, the hand of the poet shapes this elusive force into an active presence as the wind assumes a human form, mischievously performing its vital environmental function before the child. A trope under fire (indeed, some would regard her brother's programmatic avoidance of it in *Lyrical Ballads* as an integral part of a growing Romantic revolution), personification nevertheless enlivens and unifies Dorothy's poem.[9] But of course she could get away with this aesthetic collusion because the stakes were inevitably low. She wrote her poem ostensibly for a child, and it would obviously be greeted with uncomplicated delight when eventually found tucked away in William's 1815 volume. This somewhat *de trop* poetic device, however, is our way into the poem's ecological subtext, an innocuous enough entry to be sure, but one which also underscores Dorothy's ability to preserve a childlike wonder for the natural world in the wake of a mature acceptance of its destructive processes.

And in fact, play expands exponentially in the second and third stanzas as the wind makes its way through a natural setting suddenly sprung into anthropomorphic life, complete with a Dorothy Wordsworthian domestic slant.

He will suddenly stop in a cunning nook
And rings a sharp larum:—but if you should look
There's nothing to see but a cushion of snow,

Round as a pillow and whiter than milk
And softer than if it were cover'd with silk.

Sometimes he'll hide in the cave of a rock;
Then whistle as shrill as a buzzard cock;
—But seek him and what shall you find in his place
Nothing but silence and empty space
Save in a corner a heap of dry leaves
That he's left for a bed for beggars or thieves. (9–19)

Following the poem's droll logic, we quickly come to the conclusion that children, not "Scholars," are in a position to understand the language of paradox. The wind rings shrilly (notice also the structural symmetry of the two stanzas) leaving only cushions of snow or heaps of dry leaves as proofs of its continuously absent presence. Obviously Dorothy's having a bit of fun here, although it is interesting to note that her fanciful depiction of the wind's activities differs rather markedly from the "project" of the Grasmere journals as succinctly described by Margaret Homans. Dorothy's "faith," Homans writes, "is that her language can and should do no more than name the individual objects of perception. She aspires to an absolute transparency of language" (*Women Writers* 56). There's nothing particularly "transparent" about the language of the above two stanzas—I doubt we regularly think of nooks as "cunning," for example.

And yet, we must take Dorothy's play seriously if we are to understand the poem's quietly insistent ecological purpose, which begins to reveal itself in the fourth stanza, the halfway point of the poem:

As soon as 'tis daylight tomorrow with me
You shall go to the orchard & there you will see
That he has been there, & made a great rout,
And cracked the branches, & strew'd them about:
Heaven grant that he spare but that one upright twig
That look'd up at the sky so proud & big
All last summer, as well you know
Studded with apples, a beautiful shew! (20–27)

We are suddenly in a real world of time, and we might even notice that we are indoors in the act of contemplating the outdoors. This of course becomes clear in the next stanza when Dorothy reminds a potentially frightened boy that they are "snug and warm" in a cottage whose walls are "tighter than Molly's new cloak" (33, 37). In a sense, we come down to earth in the second half of the poem, without, however, leaving a world of play, Dove Cottage acting as the child's anchor, nurse, and guide, as the last stanza confirms:

> Come now we'll to bed, and when we are there
> He may work his own will, & what shall we care.
> He may knock at the door—we'll not let him in
> May drive at the windows—we'll laugh at his din
> Let him seek his own home wherever it be
> Here's a canny warm house for Johnny and me. (38–43)

The homeless wind is sent packing, and a young boy is free to enjoy a pleasant night's sleep in a "canny warm house," utterly secure from nature's ravages. Dorothy moves inexorably towards this conclusion, shutting out in the process not only the wind but possibly the Ecocritic as well. For hasn't she chosen one setting over another? Doesn't she entice us (as well as the boy) with the warm glow of a domestic environment? The poem certainly lends itself to such an interpretation; however, we should also be on our guard against a potentially limiting Cartesian reading strategy.[10] For as I have already argued in my chapter on the Grasmere journals, Dorothy's was a domestic ecology, and here it emerges in the form of a children's poem.

In 1806 (the year we believe the poem was composed), Dorothy could boast of her experience helping to raise children. And here we might wish to remind ourselves of the educational "system" she followed in 1797, since little Basil Montagu, who was under Dorothy and William's care at that time, would have been roughly the same age as the boy in this poem. "You ask to be informed of our system respecting Basil," Dorothy wrote to her friend Jane Marshall, proceeding to tell her that

> it is a very simple one, so simple that in this age of systems you will hardly be likely to follow it. We teach him nothing at present but what he learns from the evidence of his senses. He has an insatiable curiosity which we are always careful to satisfy to the best of our ability. It is directed to everything he sees, the sky, the fields, trees, shrubs, corn, the making of tools, carts, &c &c &c. He knows his letters, but we have not attempted any further step in the path of *book learning*. Our grand study has been to make him *happy* in which we have not been altogether disappointed. . . . (*Early Years* 180)

Dorothy and William's hands-off approach to Basil's education reveals a nascent belief in the efficacy of ecosystems. He learns simply by being in his environment, by engaging holistically with his surroundings.

From the vantage point of Dorothy's letter of 1797, then, "An address" might appear to represent a turning away from holistic pedagogy as language effectively replaces experience. She explains nature's processes to Johnny, and that she does so poetically suggests a descent into "*book learning*." And yet, Dorothy has immersed herself so thoroughly in the Grasmerean ecosystem that she ultimately bridges the gap between the seemingly opposed worlds of the verbal and the experiential, artfully introducing a young boy to the broader horizon of nature's processes through poetry, the green language.

With this in mind, let us reconsider Dove Cottage's role in the poem. As I have already suggested, we are possibly inside the cottage from the out-set—or at least, we come to this realization during the act of reading. The Wordsworths, however, had perceived the dwelling's significance for their lives almost immediately upon discovering it towards the end of 1799. More than a simple domestic space, Dove Cottage became the centre from which they explored their new environment, a synecdoche for Grasmere itself and thus a vital component of the "Unity entire" William describes in "Home at Grasmere." Dove Cottage retains its symbolic power in "An address"—but in a refracted form. Indeed, its rhetorical position in the poem as a kind of absent presence (much like the wind itself) clarifies Jonathan Bate's point that an ecosystem does not have a centre but rather exists (and survives) as a "network of relations" (*Song* 107). This is the poem's subtext—or rather, Dorothy quietly imparts this knowledge to the young boy while addressing him in a high wind.

The poem's language is also subtly consistent. We recall that Dorothy puts Johnny to bed with a reference to their "canny warm house," a vernacular expression that on a linguistic level resembles her earlier description of the wind's favourite "cunning nook." Of course, this could be nothing more than a coincidence, an example of a linguistic surplus that perhaps also takes in Dorothy's reference to the "cave of a rock." In fact, though, this concordance of language reveals the poem's inner coherence, even at the basic level of consonant and vowel, its all-encompassing belief in the idea of dwelling. The poem, then, concludes in the warm centre of Dove Cottage but like the wind itself possesses a kind of wild energy, compelling us back into its living network of language in what we might think of as a circulatory reading experience. That we can actually locate the poem's network of language suggests its fidelity to the concept of an ecosystem. Perhaps more important though, it means that the boy encounters the Grasmerean ecosystem first-hand through language. For wherever he turns, he finds the real—as well as potential—dwellings of Grasmere, Dove Cottage representing but one of them. Dorothy even somewhat audaciously points out that the homeless wind himself creates a home for the genuine outcasts of a community ("beggars or thieves") by heaping the scattered leaves into beds. Witnessing the wind's presence through the aeolian music of Dorothy's words (for surely she would have recited her poem to him), Johnny discovers the vitality of ecosystems.

I have said that "An address to a Child in a high wind" lacks the self-reflexive qualities of some of the more famous aeolian poems of the Romantic period. We might have noticed, however, Dorothy's more intimate use of apostrophe in the second half of the fourth stanza:

> Heaven grant that he spare but that one upright twig
> That look'd up at the sky so proud & big
> All last summer, as well you know
> Studded with apples, a beautiful shew! (24–27)

Dorothy continues to address Johnny—but from an experienced perspective. For while the boy lives in the moment (captured rhetorically in the poem's abrupt opening, a breathless series of questions concerning the wind's whereabouts), Dorothy takes the long view as she remembers—and perhaps longs for—the tree's summery abundance while simultaneously fearing for its well-being the next day. It is a deceptively complicated passage, and characteristically Wordsworthian in its merging of past, present, and future, perhaps even reminding us of Hyman Eigerman's poetic transformations of Dorothy's prose. The stanza certainly feels as if it might have had its origin in the Grasmere journals, where, as we have seen, trees figure prominently. And yet Dorothy's spontaneous act of prayer fits seamlessly into the overall movement of the poem, extending its ecological reach while keeping Johnny securely in a world of play. The poem's fourth stanza, then, illuminates a crucial aspect of Dorothy's relationship to the natural world as she acknowledges her inability to control the forces of nature. That she does so in a poem with such a clear as well as attractively subtle pedagogical purpose quietly looks forward to the subversive methodology of the ecologist.[11] "[W]ith a gentle hand / Touch,——for there is a Spirit in the woods" (53–54).

My reference to William's poem "Nutting" reminds us that William and Dorothy were engaged in a constant poetic dialogue; indeed, most consider the "dearest Maiden" invoked at the end of "Nutting" to be Dorothy herself. One of Dorothy's other earlier poems, "Grasmere—A Fragment,"

invokes not only a crucial period in the Wordsworths' lives, but also a crucial poem—William's "Home at Grasmere."[12] Karl Kroeber has described
"Home at Grasmere" as William's "longest poem about poetry" ("'Home at
Grasmere'" 140). "Grasmere—A Fragment" is decidedly not about poetry,
although we do discover poetry—that is, William's poetry—deep inside the
poem itself, an unobtrusive sequestering of language that has everything to
do with her environmental perspective. It is unlike William's poem in other
ways, too, however, as Susan Levin has demonstrated:

> The joys and sorrows of the choice [to pass her womanhood in a com-
> munity of writing that was centered around her brother] described
> in "Grasmere—A Fragment" become more obvious if Dorothy's final
> version of her arrival at Grasmere with William, her first view of
> "that dear abode" is contrasted with William's version in "Home at
> Grasmere." Their similar vocabularies include "wanderers," a "shed,"
> and "inmates." . . . But his description corresponds more closely
> to letters written to Coleridge . . . and is probably a more faith-
> ful account. . . . According to William in the letters and "Home at
> Grasmere," they arrived in the village during the early evening. . . . In
> Dorothy's poem they arrive early enough for her to take a walk, a seem-
> ingly independent action that in her poem's telling actually indicates
> dependence and passivity. (151)

Levin's analysis introduces us to a curious feature of the poem—its
seeming lack of concern for factual accuracy. Indeed, at several points it
engages in out-and-out fantasy. The speaker, however (or Dorothy, as I will
refer to her from now on), clearly knows this, and in fact knowledge emerges
very quickly as perhaps the poem's central preoccupation.

I seem to have plunged headlong into the discussion, but before starting
over again at the beginning I would like to point out that Levin's comparison
of "Grasmere—A Fragment" with "Home at Grasmere" gestures toward her
basic thesis, one which I believe needs refutation.

> While settling down in Grasmere fulfilled Dorothy's long-held dream, it
> brought with it the knowledge of missed past and future opportunities.
> Life at Grasmere both encouraged and inhibited a woman trying to find
> an identity as a writer among men of genius. (154)

"Grasmere—A Fragment" opens in the present tense with a general
description of Grasmere Vale and the cottage at Town End.

Peaceful our valley, fair and green,
And beautiful her cottages,
Each in its nook, its sheltered hold,
Or underneath its tuft of trees

Many and beautiful they are;
But there is *one* that I love best,
A lowly shed, in truth it is,
A brother of the rest.

Yet when I sit on rock or hill,
Down looking on the valley fair,
That Cottage with its clustering trees
Summons my heart; it settles there. (1–12)

Like "Home at Grasmere," "Grasmere—A Fragment" begins on a hill, but where the former opens on a prospect taken from memory, here Dorothy presents the scene as a recurring condition, for Dorothy is celebrating the fact that she has a home. This doesn't mean that she treats time cavalierly, however, and in fact the poem divides itself temporally into two roughly equal parts. The first part (comprised of ten stanzas) is devoted to a present-tense description of the Cottage and its environs, while the second part (comprised of twelve stanzas) focuses on the day of their arrival, which we happen know was December 20th, 1799. The poem's first half, then, acts as a kind of prelude to the story that follows—the story she and her brother never tired of telling.[13]

"The poets who are at one with nature are [in Schiller's terms] . . . 'naïve,' while those who are conscious of themselves and their own separation from nature are 'sentimental.'" (*Romantic* 103). So Jonathan Bate reminds us in the midst of his brief discussion of "Home at Grasmere." Pastoral is the "key 'sentimental' form" (according to Bate via Schiller), which means that "Home at Grasmere" is an example of sentimental poetry. It's not a lesser poem as a result, however, and indeed for Bate plays a crucial role in William's astonishingly quick transformation into a "naïve" poet.

> Having explored the vale in *Home at Grasmere*, Wordsworth was able by
> the end of the year to enter into the life of a representative inhabitant of
> the vale, to enter fully into the feelings of the shepherd. (104)

Bate is referring to "Michael," and I have incorporated his description of William's relationship to Schiller's influential categories at this point in my discus-

sion for two reasons. First, it situates "Home at Grasmere" within the broader
continuum of poetry William had been creating since his arrival (which would
also include his "Poems on the Naming of Places") and thus illustrates his keen
interest in poetical development—a development that had everything to do
with living in Grasmere. This is in marked contrast to Dorothy, who I would
argue was not interested in "developing" at all, at least in any traditional sense
of the term, either as a writer or a poet. She simply wanted to share a home
with her brother, the achievement of which set her writing in motion (as soon,
that is, as she experienced William's first protracted absence). For Dorothy,
writing was a truly natural activity, and certainly didn't exist in relation to a
greater plan or purpose. Interestingly, however, Schiller's categories undergo a
transformation when applied to her poetry, which also grew out of her experiences in Grasmere. For as we are about to see (and this is my second reason for referring to Bate's reading of William's poem in this context), Dorothy
describes her home and homecoming in naively sentimental terms.

    After briefly entertaining the idea that some might prefer another cot-
tage or dwelling ("Others there are whose small domain / Of fertile fields and
hedgerows green / Might more seduce a wanderer's mind" [13–15]), Dorothy
momentarily forsakes her prospect. "—I love that house because it is / The
very Mountains' child" (19–20), she exclaims, an apostrophe that results in a
brilliantly fanciful description of the landscape surrounding her home and its
relationship to the elements:

> Fields hath it of its own, green fields,
> But they are rocky steep, and bare;
> Their fence is of the mountain stone,
> And moss and lichen flourish there.
>
> And when the storm comes from the North
> It lingers near that pastoral spot,
> And, piping through the mossy walls,
> It seems delighted with its lot.
>
> And let it take its own delight;
> And let it range the pastures bare;
> Until it reach that group of trees,
> —It may not enter there! (21–32)

    It is almost as if we have returned to the childlike world of "An address
to a Child in a high wind," and yet here there are no children. Actually,

Johnny could very well be indoors as Dorothy sits and takes in the view of their cottage and its surroundings, an inversion of the situation in the former poem, since of course "An address" finds Dorothy and Johnny cozily ensconced inside the cottage. Initially this seems to inspire decidedly unadorned description; for the fields (and notice Dorothy's particularly effective use of *epanalepsis* in the line where that word twice appears) "are rocky steep, and bare," and their "fence is of the mountain stone." In other words, she begins by emphasizing a simple—even minimalist—natural world, which the personified storm in all its piping glory attempts to intrude upon, looking ridiculous in the process, of course. (Like the wind in "An address," the storm is sent packing—in this instance back to the North.)

The first part of the poem concludes with a consolidation of sorts—as its penultimate stanza demonstrates:

> A green unfading grove it is,
> Skirted with many a lesser tree,
> Hazel & holly, beech and oak,
> A bright and flourishing company. (33–36)

Fact and fancy merge seamlessly in this quatrain. For Dorothy's description of the "unfading grove" (and we derive an almost incantatory pleasure from repeating that first line over and over to ourselves) leads to a more precise—as well as a particularly well-balanced—delineation of its flora, "Hazel & holly, beech and oak." The quatrain then ends on a quietly visionary note with the Grasmerean shrubs and trees illuminated seemingly from within.

Dorothy's present-tense description of the "unfading grove" seems to unearth an unfading memory, inaugurating the second part of the poem:

> When first I saw that dear abode,
> It was a lovely winter's day:
> After a night of perilous storm
> The west wind ruled with gentle sway;
>
> A day so mild, it might have been
> The first day of the gladsome spring;
> The robins warbled, and I heard
> One solitary throstle sing. (41–48)

Susan Levin notes that "[in his letters to Coleridge] William includes mention of several days of delightful sightseeing," while here "Dorothy speaks of a 'perilous storm' of the preceding night, emphasizing by contrast the beauty and rest found in Grasmere" (151). Interestingly, however, those "several days of delightful sightseeing" do not inform William's *poetic* account of the journey in "Home at Grasmere," perhaps because having made a fresh start on *The Recluse* project he is keen to underscore its heroic aspect:

> Bleak season was it, turbulent and bleak,
> When hitherward we journeyed, and on foot,
> Through bursts of sunshine and through flying snows,
> Paced the long Vales, how long they were, and yet
> How fast that length of way was left behind,
> Wensley's long Vale and Sedbergh's naked heights. (218–23)

Dorothy and William's contrasting descriptions seem to put them on either side of the Continental Divide separating the Burkean categories of the Beautiful and the Sublime. Closer inspection, however, reveals similarities on a deeper, ecological level. (I will not, then, be analyzing the two poems in relation to Burke's categories.[14]) That is to say, both William and Dorothy freely manipulate past experience, as the biographical record makes clear, in order to re-introduce themselves perpetually to a known environment.

It might therefore be significant that the temporal shift from present to past between the first and second parts of Dorothy's poem results in an intensifying—as opposed to a change—of rhetorical procedure. We already know that she envisions a solitary walk, one that did not actually take place:

> A Stranger, Grasmere, in thy Vale,
> All faces then to me unknown,
> I left my sole companion-friend
> To wander out alone. (49–52)

But this fabricated walk is a vital aspect of her story, and we mustn't forget that she ultimately tells a story. We are, in fact, lured along with our protagonist into a new, living environment, our biographies of the Wordsworths slipping away as we fall under the spell of Dorothy's account of her peripatetic adventures.

> Lured by a little winding path,
> I quitted soon the public road,
> A smooth and tempting path it was,
> By sheep and shepherds trod.

Eastward, toward the lofty hills,
This pathway led me on
Until I reached a stately Rock,
With velvet moss o'ergrown.

With russet oak and tufts of fern
Its top was richly garlanded;
Its sides adorned with eglantine
Bedropp'd with hips of glossy red.

There, too, in many a sheltered chink
The foxglove's broad leaves flourished fair,
And silver birch whose purple twigs
Bend to the softest breathing air.

Beneath that Rock my course I stayed,
And, looking to its summit high,
"Thou wear'st, said I, "a splendid garb,
Here winter keeps his revelry." (53–72)

We might have noticed that in the previously quoted stanza Dorothy addresses Grasmere directly ("A Stranger, Grasmere, in thy Vale, / All faces then to me unknown"), an intimate gesture that momentarily blurs past and present as she pauses to consider the Vale she now knows so well. Of course, implicitly she treats the Vale as a living thing from the very beginning. Situated as it is, however, just after that point when present becomes past, her unambiguously intimate apostrophe not only subtly colours our sense of the first part of the poem; it also prepares us for what follows.

And what follows is a splendidly playful—but also deeply felt—dialogue between Dorothy and a personified environment, an environment she initially describes in precise but also lush detail. Dorothy's keen eye for English flora comes to the fore here, but she also cannot resist description of a more purplish variety, which manifests itself quite literally in the "purple twigs" of the "silver birches." We then watch with Dorothy as those same twigs "Bend to the softest breathing air" (a perfectly modulated line that should quell any doubts about her poetical abilities), and in fact their loving surrender signals the end of the description proper. Perhaps inspired by her own subtly anthropomorphic language (for why shouldn't we think of the poem's events as also having taken place at the moment of creation?), Dorothy turns to greet a brilliantly bespangled winter landscape. We'll pick up where we left off, stopping just before the poem's final stanza.

> "Full long a dweller on the Plains,
> I griev'd when summer days were gone;
> No more I'll grieve; for Winter here
> Hath pleasure gardens of his own.
>
> What need of flowers? The splendid moss
> Is gayer than an April mead;
> More rich its hues of various green,
> Orange, and gold, & glittering red."
>
> —Beside that gay and lovely Rock
> There came with merry voice
> A foaming streamlet glancing by;
> It seemed to say "Rejoice!" (73–84)

In a recent ecocritical consideration of the Romantic apostrophe, Helena Feder has suggested that "apostrophe functions as an anti-anthropomorphic device, for as philosopher Edmund Husserl discerned, associative empathy enables us to escape solipsism" (57). Her primary example is Shelley's "Ode to the West Wind," and her findings are worth quoting in more detail, since they represent an especially fine example of ecological thinking.

> We escape [solipsism] through Shelley's poetic sympathy, through the poet's synchronicity of senses and rhythms, through reciprocity, through the recognition of interconnectedness. In the words of Gary Snyder, ecology is "a problem of love, not the humanistic love of the West—but a love that extends to the animals, rocks, dirt, all of it. Without this love we can end . . . with an uninhabitable place" (*The Real Work* 4). (57–58)

Dorothy and William Wordsworth solve the ecological "problem" of love through a radical form of apostrophe that allows for a complete communion (through human-centred communication) with Grasmere Vale, resulting in what James McKusick defines as a "human ecology."[15] For William's poetic treatment of their journey in "Home at Grasmere," while obviously different in some respects, mirrors Dorothy's. (Or is it the other way around?

In the Grasmerean ecosystem influence must be understood as a reciprocal process.)

>   . . . The naked Trees,
> The icy brooks, as on we passed, appeared
> To question us. "Whence come ye? to what end?"
> They seemed to say; "What would ye," said the shower,
> "Wild Wanderers, whither through my dark domain?"
> The sunbeam said, "be happy." (229–34)

Like Dorothy, William describes this encounter in somewhat equivocal terms; the naked Trees and icy brooks appear to question them (while for Dorothy the streamlet appeared to say "Rejoice!"), which suggests that he has adopted a knowledgeable, ultimately "sentimental" perspective. And yet, by the end of the passage Nature's voice (speaking through a phenomenal world of multifarious things—a shower, a sunbeam) commands them to "be happy." That is to say, William's description unfetters itself as it proceeds, giving way to an apparently unmediated dialogue between the Wordsworths and a new environment. (Perhaps this very dialogue even helped inspire William's "naïve" poem, "Michael"? We may or may not be able to prove this, but one thing is clear: William's poetry always gestures beyond itself to a boundless poetical future.)

This brings us, in fact, to a key difference between William and Dorothy's environmental perspectives, which I would like to approach through the last stanza of "Grasmere—A Fragment." We recall that the penultimate stanza concludes with the streamlet commanding her—or at least appearing to command her—to "Rejoice!" Interestingly, that jubilant exclamation represents the climax of the poem. From an aesthetic point of view this seems right (in musical terms it's rather like concluding a string quartet on the tonic after hectic, modulated development), but the somber note on which the poem seems to end might suggest other things as well.

> My youthful wishes all fulfill'd,
> Wishes matured by thoughtful choice,
> I stood an Inmate of this vale
> How *could* I but rejoice? (85–88)

Susan Levin hears a "still, sad music" in this stanza ("Tintern Abbey" 92), and her particularly fine-tuned analysis of its tonal ambivalence reveals many nuances.

In nineteenth-century usage the word [inmate] was not applied to prisoners, but it was used to indicate a patient in an insane asylum or a person not properly belonging to the place he inhabits. . . . And the last line of Dorothy's poem, though it may echo "A poet could not but be gay" in William's "Daffodils," does so ambivalently, with a characteristic question. The structure of the sentence—"How *could* I but rejoice?"—brings up the possibility that the speaker in fact does not rejoice, that the life described is sad and unfulfilled. (153)

For a well-versed reader of Dorothy's poetry, Levin's suggestions (which she has skillfully qualified, but which nevertheless emerge as more than mere suggestions) bring to mind her later work, particularly those poems that came after her complete breakdown in 1829. "Thoughts on my sickbed," for example, finds the poet a literal "prisoner" in her "lonely room" (45), although she manages to escape temporarily—thanks in part to her Bard-Brother-Friend's poetry (48). The poem in fact concludes with a direct reference to "Tintern Abbey," even incorporating one of its most crucial words—"motion"—into its last stanza. Perhaps, then, Dorothy's future as the prisoner-poet has unwittingly cast its dark spectral rays backward on Levin's interpretation of a poem possibly composed as early as 1805, and in fact this is what I suggest. Similarly, I would also suggest that the question with which Dorothy concludes her poem is not inherently ambiguous, although it certainly might lend itself to a skeptical interpretation. (Just as for some the rhetorical questions that crop up in rather unexpected places in "Tintern Abbey" point to the poet's less than "Roman confidence" in Nature [*The Prelude*, Book II 459].) We must also, however, grant the question its measure of joy.[16] Indeed, it and the entire stanza's careful balancing of potential pleasures and pains recalls a passage from "Home at Grasmere" itself.

> Joy spreads and sorrow spreads; and this whole Vale
> Home of untutored Shepherds as it is,
> Swarms with sensation, as with gleams of sunshine,
> Shadows or breezes, scents or sounds. . . . (664–67)

And this brings us to one of the more curious features of Dorothy's poem. It begins in the present tense and concludes in the past tense, but at no point do we encounter the future tense. We might say, then, that there is no future in "Grasmere—A Fragment." "Home at Grasmere," on the other hand, acquires its shape through a continual evocation of the future (although it begins with a sharply realized memory) and then concludes with the great "Prospectus," certainly the most provocative poetic statement of intent William ever made. We might say, then, that there is only the future in "Home at Grasmere," which might account for the restlessness we detect lurking almost everywhere under its rhetorically spectacular surface. "But 'tis not to enjoy, for this alone / That we exist," the poet exclaims just before launching into the "Prospectus."

> . . . no, something must be done.
> I must not walk in unreproved delight
> These narrow bounds and think of nothing more,
> No duty that looks further and no care. (875–79)

William gestures here rather anxiously towards the future, but of course the poem also appears to exist perpetually in the year 1800, an all-encompassing spot of time located in the always-receding past of the present-tense moment. In other words, he seems to want to be everywhere at once (although David Simpson argues that he is in fact nowhere at all[17]). Kenneth Johnston has even perceptively pointed out that "[i]f all its linguistic peculiarities were generalized into a single compressed sentence, they would collapse all tenses into one: 'Once upon a time I am living happily ever after'" (*Wordsworth and* 88). We might doubt one can actually achieve such a condition, but with "Home at Grasmere" William had raised the poetic stakes beyond even his own formidable reach, which is perhaps why it was left unpublished until 1888, long after his death.

Conversely, it seems that Dorothy did not strive enough, that she was simply too content to exist in the shadow of her brilliant brother's talents, leaving her in a kind of perpetual state of arrested (artistic) development. "Grasmere—A Fragment" re-enacts the process of Dorothy's journey to dubious contentment in the form of a story, one that concludes in the past, shutting the door on the future in the process. For some, then (and certainly for Susan Levin), that last stanza represents a kind of terrible crystallization, an ironic expression of "joy" (a "central and recurrent term in . . . Romantic vocabulary," as M. H. Abrams has pointed out[18]) that can only lead to the silencing of song.

But have we listened closely enough to Dorothy's music? In fact, I would argue that "Grasmere—A Fragment" is a differently pitched Ode to Joy. Less obviously celebratory than "Home at Grasmere" (but even its sometimes deafening strains of joy cannot completely drown out an antithetical countermelody always threatening to take precedence), it nevertheless remains in control as it dispenses with the future in order to emphasize the present. Even its last line, inflected as it is in the form of a question in the past tense, possesses an inner momentum that recalls the joyful strains of the poem's present-tense opening. This is not to say that it concludes in simple exultation: we cannot hear the "eager sound" of wings as birds "shape / Orb after orb their course still round and round / Above the area of the Lake, their own / Adopted region, girding it about / In wanton repetition. . . ." ("Home at Grasmere" 292–96). But if we listen closely enough, we might hear a measured breathing which is the sound of a natural poet rooted in her environment longing for nothing.

Levin conjectures that Dorothy composed "Floating Island at Hawkshead, An Incident in the schemes of Nature" in the late 1820s, some twenty years after writing "An address" and "Grasmere—A Fragment." Shelley had grieved for the "Poet of Nature" back in 1816 in his sonnet "To Wordsworth," and clearly Dorothy had settled down with her brother to a life of political and religious orthodoxy long before she wrote this poem. "Floating Island at Hawkshead," however, demonstrates that her understanding of nature, as well as her knowledge of the craft of poetry, had only intensified with the passing of time.[19]

As the second half of its title implies, "Floating Island at Hawkshead" is (ostensibly) a narrative poem. It begins, however, on a declarative note:

Harmonious Powers with Nature work
On sky, earth, river, lake, and sea:
Sunshine and storm, whirlwind and breeze
All in one duteous task agree. (1–4)

This beautifully balanced quatrain (notice the poise of that third line, for example, its medial caesura suggesting the shape of the stanza as a whole) acts as a kind of prologue to the "incident" that follows at the same time that it represents the essence of the poem itself. Thus, on one level Dorothy's resulting narrative illustrates, or proves, the truth of her opening claim. On another level, however, the narrative springs forth from this descriptive opening stanza (a little world unto itself) before ultimately collapsing back into it. In fact, Dorothy's rhetorical strategy—here and throughout the poem—mirrors the mysterious natural phenomenon we are about to encounter.

And we encounter this phenomenon in the form of a story. Or at least so we naturally think as we read the second stanza:

Once did I see a slip of earth,
By throbbing waves long undermined,

Loosed from its hold;—*how* no one knew
But all might see it float, obedient to the wind. (5–8)

Dorothy begins in the classic manner ("once upon a time"), but strictly speaking her story comprises only two-and-a-half lines of verse; for the caesura in the seventh line signals a shift in direction—that is, the end of the narrative proper, although we might not sense this immediately. Moving into the third stanza, however, we *are* likely to notice Dorothy's beautiful and ultimately fitting use of rhetorical schemes as she repeats and re-balances two words we have already encountered.

Might see it, from the verdant shore
Dissevered float upon the Lake,
Float, with its crest of trees adorned
On which the warbling birds their pastime take. (9–12)

Dissevered thus, the two stanzas reveal a seemingly capricious poetics. The personal pronoun "I" inaugurates the story in the first stanza, but then just as quickly disappears, never in fact to return again. Moving through the next stanza, we encounter a shift in tense from past to present that happens to coincide with the island's swimming into our ken. And here, of course, at the edge of the floating island, we realize that the story itself (such as it was) concluded before the end of the previous stanza. The two stanzas, however, are inextricably linked through Dorothy's careful use of rhetorical schemes.

As I have already suggested, the uncanny and yet utterly natural phenomenon Dorothy describes clarifies her methodology (and vice versa, of course). Let's step on to the island itself, then, and experience the entire process, for as we will soon discover, the incident that inspired the poem is actually a perpetually occurring natural process. Perhaps fittingly (given the example of the Grasmere journals), Dorothy continues to concentrate on the "warbling birds" that congregate at the end of the third stanza before proceeding to consider the island's self-sustaining—and ultimately self-immolating—population:

Food, shelter, safety there they find
There berries ripen, flowerets bloom;
There insects live their lives—and die:
A peopled *world* it is;—in size a tiny room. (13–16)

We have already encountered this stanza.[20] Transplanting it back into its natural environment, however, illuminates the aesthetic side of Dorothy's domestic ecology. Thinking himself in terms of aesthetics, Jonathan Bate has suggested that

> verse-making is language's most direct path of return to the *oikos*, the place of dwelling, because metre itself—a quiet but persistent music, a recurring cycle, a heartbeat—is an answering to nature's own rhythms, an echoing of the earth itself. (*Song* 76)

Here, at the very centre of Dorothy's poem, metre and form unite in a stanza that uncannily answers to nature's own rhythms through a process of complete communion. For, etymologically speaking, stanzas are themselves "tiny rooms," and in just three lines this one describes the entire life cycle of the island. The verses are notably unsentimental ("insects live their lives—and die"); a colon, however, connects them to the stanza's concluding line, a controlled burst of metaphor: "A people *world* it is;—in size a tiny room." Rhythmically, that last line repeats the process enacted in the previous verses, its rising and falling cadence (as well as its expanding and contracting diction) mimicking in its measured breathing the life cycle of the island Dorothy has just captured poetically.

The poem, in fact, appears to eddy here at the midway point, caught in the vortex of its own circular rhetorical energies. And yet, just as the poem does not actually tell a story, so it does not actually have a centre. Neither, however, are we approaching (as we might now think we are) the cliff's edge of Deconstruction. For doesn't "Floating Island at Hawkshead" describe—as well as itself behave like—an ecosystem? Far from eddying, then, the poem is ready to spring forward, ceaselessly, as it turns out, and so are we—that is, after we have paused to reconsider Kroeber's definition of an ecosystem as a "constantly self-transforming continuity" (*Ecological* 55).

This is how Dorothy concludes:

> And thus through many seasons' space
> This little Island may survive
> But Nature, though we mark her not,
> Will take away—may cease to give.
>
> Perchance when you are wandering forth
> Upon some vacant sunny day
> Without an object, hope, or fear,
> Thither your eyes may turn—the Isle is passed away.

Buried beneath the glittering Lake!
Its place no longer to be found,
Yet the lost fragments shall remain,
To fertilize some other ground. (17–28)

In the fourth stanza, Dorothy traces the life cycle of the island's diminutive population; here she charts the inevitable demise of the island itself—and in rather intricate fashion. In fact, it is a three-stage—as well as a tidy three-stanza—process. For after acknowledging Nature's fickleness (she "*Will* take away—*may* cease to give"), she turns and addresses her readers directly, imagining us wandering forth idyllically in the future on a vacant sunny day "[w]ithout an object, hope, or fear." But we arrive too late on the scene—the "Isle is passed away." With such knowledge, however, comes abundant recompense, since Dorothy concludes by informing us that the island's "lost fragments shall remain, / To fertilize some other ground." Taken as a whole, Dorothy's description of the entire cycle represents a classic early manifestation of ecological thinking, the very epitome of Kroeber's definition.

Clearly I am reading Dorothy's poem paradigmatically, a methodology I embrace as a means of remaining true to the role McKusick argues the Romantic poets played in "creating a new, holistic way of perceiving the natural world. . . ." (11). I also, however, wish to remain true to the concept of an ecosystem, which, "is now regarded as a much more chaotic and unstable structure than the classic scientific understanding of the 'balance of nature' might have suggested" (McKusick 18). Itself a "chaotic and unstable structure," "Floating Island at Hawkshead" threatens to drown in the wake of its rhetorical excesses, but of course doesn't. The art of reading the poem, then, involves our making sense of it as a constantly self-transforming continuous structure. It is always on the verge of becoming something else—an argument, a narrative, or series of narratives, even possibly a parody,[21] yet retains its shape as a discrete work, in part because of its formal coherence. Indeed, it is one of Dorothy's most accomplished poems. Like her other works, however, it ultimately exists beyond itself. It is not a self-contained lyrical effusion (like, say, "I Wandered Lonely as a Cloud"), but rather a textual *environment*. Poet (a muted presence to begin with), subject matter (the island in all it incarnations), reader (a potential future inhabitant)—the poem continuously flourishes through their interrelationship. To experience such an environment is to witness first-hand the ecopoetics, or Harmonious Powers, that with nature work to create a genuinely ecological poetry.

Chapter Four

"More Allied to Human Life": Dorothy Wordsworth's Communion with the Dead

The first part of my title comes from Dorothy Wordsworth's description of a funeral she attended (at John Dawson's farm, just south of Dove Cottage) on September 3, 1800. "The dead person 56 years of age buried by the parish," she records in her Grasmere journals:

> —the coffin was neatly lettered & painted black & covered with a decent cloth. They set the corpse down at the door & while we stood within the threshold the men with their hats off sang with decent & solemn countenances a verse of a funeral psalm. The corpse was then borne down the hill & they sang till they had got past the Town-end. I was affected to tears while we stood in the house, the coffin lying before me. There were no near kindred, no children. When we got out of the dark house the sun was shining & the prospect looked so divinely beautiful as I never saw it. It seemed more sacred than I had ever seen it, & yet more allied to human life. The green fields, neighbours of the churchyard, were green as possible & with the brightness of the sunshine looked quite Gay. I thought she was going to a quiet spot & I could not help weeping very much. (20)

The second part of my title was inspired by a passage from the first of William Wordsworth's *Essays upon Epitaphs*—a passage that in my view will help clarify Dorothy's funeral experience, and indeed might help us better understand her relationship with the dead (and death) in general:

> The sensations of pious cheerfulness, which attend the celebration of the sabbath-day in rural places, are profitably chastised by the sight of the graves of kindred and friends, gathered together in that general home towards which the thoughtful yet happy spectators themselves

are journeying. Hence a parish-church, in the stillness of the country, is a visible centre of a community of the living and the dead; a point to which are habitually referred the nearest concerns of both.[1] (330)

It seems William wrote the first of his *Essays upon Epitaphs* between the end of 1809 and the beginning of 1810—not that long, in fact, after Dorothy wrote *A Narrative Concerning George and Sarah Green of the Parish of Grasmere*. Dorothy was in the midst of composing her narrative barely a month after George and Sarah Green perished on March 19, 1808 while trying to return home to Easedale from a sale in Langdale.[2] A consideration of the *Narrative* of the Greens will comprise a significant portion of this chapter, an alternative title for which could be "The Greening of the Green Narrative." Due to the scope of my consideration of Dorothy's relationship with the dead, however, a more all-encompassing title seems appropriate. Nevertheless, readers might wish to keep this alternative title in mind, particularly as it invokes the ecocritical perspective from which I will continue to examine Dorothy's work.

William's description of a parish-church as "a visible centre of a community of the living and the dead" gestures toward a Grasmerean culture of death; read in conjunction with her other Grasmere writings, however, Dorothy's narrative of the Greens immerses us in it. This is not to say that William was not interested in this culture; in fact, as Kenneth Johnston has demonstrated, Books V–IX of *The Excursion* are vitally concerned with Grasmere's dead folk as the Priest (at some length) provides an "account of persons interred in the Churchyard" (152).[3] But as Johnston has also suggested, *The Excursion*'s relationship to the *Recluse* project may have determined some of its larger concerns:

> Although they are dead, the concentration of their stories is not upon death as such, but on death as the final shaper of our ends, the last touch which completes the form of our lives. Like William's contemporaneous "Essay upon Epitaphs," these stories dwell less upon death than on what might be said about it; each of them is in effect an epitaph, the smallest compression of the fullest story, a direction in which *The Recluse* was always tending once it began its dialectical relations with *The Prelude*, the fullest expansion of the most individual story. (*Wordsworth and* 287)

This is not the place for an examination of *The Excursion*'s relationship to *The Recluse* (or *The Prelude*); however, Johnston's evocation of the first of the *Essays upon Epitaphs* is appropriate, since William eventually incorporated it into his poem as a (very long) note.[4] Could it be that he was inspired to work once again on *The Recluse* while standing in the Grasmere church-yard contemplating the Greens' tragic fate? That was where he composed his short poem "George and Sarah Green," less than two years before writing the first of his *Essays upon Epitaphs*. Given the impact that Grasmere's dead had on *The Excursion* at this time—as well as the fact that the *Recluse* project seemed to draw everything into its orbit—it is tempting to speculate that William's elegy for the Greens had its origins in the project that haunted him (and his family) for much of his adult life. Perhaps this would explain why, as Susan Levin has suggested, the poem does not "have the straightfor-ward, substantive coherence of Dorothy's narrative" (49).[5] Whatever causes may have contributed to the creation of what de Selincourt describes as that "feeble composition" (*A Narrative* 8), it could be that William's Reclusive tendencies—which on one level manifest themselves in the project's daunt-ing conceptual framework—ironically kept him at some remove from the people of Grasmere. Dorothy's communion with Grasmere's living and dead inhabitants, on the other hand, is a direct result of her daily participation in its culture of death.

Dorothy and William's lives were of course shaped by death; the loss of their parents in childhood, early separation (itself a kind of death), and perhaps above all the drowning of their beloved brother John—these events determined the pattern of their lives, cementing the bonds of an already unbreakable relationship. But as I hope my reading of "Grasmere—A Frag-ment" in chapter three has demonstrated, Dorothy had her own sense of place, one that grew and changed over time. How did death contribute to Dorothy's continuously unfolding relationship to her environment? What happened when the "unknown" faces she recalls having encountered upon first coming to Gramsere became known to her—and then vanished?[6] In attempting to answer these questions, I do not wish to sever the established bonds of brother and sister, but rather illustrate how Dorothy's encounters with death in a particular environment moved her towards an awareness of place that was at once Romantic and communal.

I have already remarked on this chapter's human-centred orientation, but a memorable passage from one of Dorothy's letters to Catherine Clarkson should be kept in mind as a salutary reminder of her inclusive environmental perspective. It dates from the summer of 1807 (less than a year before the Greens' ill-fated journey), when the Wordsworth family had just returned from an eight-month visit at Coleorton where they had been staying as the Beaumonts' guests. The entire letter is interesting, not least of which for its detailed description of their leisurely—but not entirely pleasant—journey home, giving us another glimpse of Dorothy's tourist side. Describing Bolton Abbey, for example, Dorothy remarks that " . . . the Ruin is greatly inferior to Kirkstall; but the situation is infinitely more beautiful, a retired woody winding valley, with steep banks and rocky scars, no manufactories—no horrible Forges and yet the Forge near Kirkstall has often a very grand effect" (*Middle Years, 1806–1811* 158).[7] Her tourist perspective vanishes, however, as soon as they reach Grasmere and discover the devastating changes that have occurred in their absence.

> On our arrival here our spirits sank and our first walk in the evening was very melancholy. Many persons are dead, old Mr. Sympson, his son the parson, young George Dawson, the finest young Man in the vale, Jenny Hodgson our washerwoman, old Jenny Dockwray and a little girl Dorothy's age who never got the better of the hooping-cough which she had when we went away. (158–59)

It is a doleful and rather astonishing death toll, giving us a sense of the mortality rates in England's more remote districts in the early nineteenth century. In the very next sentence, however, she concludes her sad inventory with a consideration of the changes that have affected the non-human realm. "All the trees in Brainriggs," she notes, "are cut down, and even worse, the giant sycamore near the parsonage house, and all the finest firtrees that overtopped the steeple tower. At home we found all well; the garden very nice the roses more abundant than ever" (159). We notice that Dorothy finds relief as she shifts her attention to their home proper (where all is well), and in general her description of felled trees might not seem as emotionally charged as that which we find in, say, "The Fallen Elm," John Clare's deeply moving poetic account of a particular tree's fate that also serves as a scathing denunciation of the enclosure movement.[8] Nevertheless, her letter is notable for its judicious consideration of human and non-human loss. Having lived in Grasmere for so long, Dorothy cannot help but mourn the disappearance of people and trees.

Dorothy's reactions to death involved more than straightforward mourning, however, as an examination of her account of the funeral she attended at John Dawson's will reveal. As we have already seen, the experience provoked an intense response; she sheds tears while standing in the house, for example, and she "couldn't help weeping very much" again while outdoors considering the "quiet spot" to which the deceased is journeying. And yet, we must not forget that Dorothy attended a pauper's funeral; it is conceivable that she barely knew Susan Shacklock, "the dead person 56 years of age buried by the parish" (and who remains unnamed in the entry).[9] For in addition to weeping copiously (twice), she also mentions that the "10 men and 4 women" attending the funeral talked "sensibly and chearfully about common things," almost as if she had been a detached observer of the proceedings. In other words, Dorothy's eye for detail remains unclouded despite her tears, which is not to say that her feelings regarding this potentially faceless individual's fate were not genuine. They might have been Romantically inflected, however, and in fact this entry is similar to others in the Grasmere journals in its depiction of Dorothy's—and William's—Romantic relationship to death.

Gary Kelly has defined "Romantic death" as "the sublation of death, or meaningful death, in meaningful life" (201). Kelly's Hegelian definition emerges within a very specific argumentative context, one that I will consider more closely before turning to Dorothy's narrative of the Greens. Here, however, I am interested in exploring how this basic definition might inform our interpretation of Dorothy's funeral experience. "Sublation" is of course the key word, and Kelly points out that in "post-Revolutionary philosophy . . . [it] has the triple and paradoxical senses of 'raising up,' 'abolishing,' and 'preserving.'" (201). Perhaps we can simplify the paradox (without negating it, however) by saying that sublation involves achieving continuity in change. Turning back to Dorothy's entry, might we not say that its unnamed subject attains exactly such a state—or rather, that Dorothy's shifting diction allows her to do so? Initially described as the "dead person," Susan Shacklock next devolves into a "corpse . . . borne down the hill" before finally acquiring her female identity (she is "raised up"), at which point she merges in death with her Grasmerean surroundings in life thereby achieving a kind of immortality while simultaneously becoming part of Dorothy's subjective vision:

> When we got out of the dark house the sun was shining & the prospect looked so divinely beautiful as I never saw it. It seemed more sacred than I had ever seen it, & yet more allied to human life. The green fields, neighbours of the churchyard, were green as possible & with the brightness of the sunshine looked quite Gay. I thought she was going to a quiet spot & I could not help weeping very much. (20)

As Dorothy moves out of the dark house into the sun, death's black rays paradoxically illuminate the prospect, and in fact death has become as a kind of rejuvenating force. The green fields are now as "green as possible," while an unnamed woman achieves an identity through dying; indeed, she seems more alive than dead at this point in the entry. So while Dorothy's funeral experience concludes in quiet, tearful solitude, her tears possess a "renovating Virtue" (*The Prelude*, Book XI 260).[10] In Kelly's terms, she has found meaning in death, which results in her intensified appreciation for life.

Dorothy's account of her funeral experience is significant in part for its depiction of Grasmerean ritual; its subjective energies, however, remind us of a private realm of death existing beyond the boundaries of rural custom. Perhaps not surprisingly, Dorothy and William frequently explored this "territory" together (within the very real boundaries of Grasmere), which necessitates an examination of the role William played in the Grasmere journals' treatment of Romantic death.

The spring of 1802 marked a new creative beginning for William. Jared Curtis suggests that "[o]nly the brilliantly productive winters, 1798–1799 and 1804–1805, when work on *The Prelude* was most intense, can vie with the late winter and spring of 1802 in the amount and high quality of the verse composed" (5). William published the majority of these "spring lyrics" five years later in *Poems, in Two Volumes*, and they incurred the wrath of the critics. Byron's devastating description of these poems as "'common-place ideas' clothed 'in language not simple, but puerile . . . namby-pamby'" remains perhaps the most notorious attack, but it is also representative (qtd. in Gill *A Life* 266).[11] It seems that the majority of the English reading public were not interested in William's joyous descriptions of birds twittering and lakes glittering (to adapt language from "Written in March," the poem that triggered Byron's memorable assault). Dorothy's journals, however, fill out this springtime in William's poetic life, for in addition to giving us almost daily proof of William's creative resurgence, they also provide us with a nearly complete record of the poems he was writing at this time, some of which he never published.

Perhaps the most singular of these unpublished poems is "These chairs they have no words to utter." As metrically simple as its springtime counterparts, its mood is anything but "namby-pamby." Divided into two parts, it begins with its speaker contemplating an individual (who is essentially a projection of himself) lying "in peace on his bed, / Happy as they who are dead" (11–12).[12] It concludes, however, with a fervent but carefully modulated apostrophe, its speaker having apparently overcome his longing for death, perhaps through an act of sublation:

> O life there is about thee
> A deep delicious peace;
> I would not be without thee,

Stay, oh stay!
Yet be thou ever as now,
Sweetness and breath with the quiet of death,
Peace, peace, peace. (24–30)

Dorothy describes William "repeating the poem" to Coleridge while the three of them were out walking on April 22, explaining that it was "called to his mind by the dying away of the stunning of the Waterfall [in Easedale] when he came behind a stone" (The Grasmere journals 89). Pamela Woof suggests that the poem "was recently written" (Dorothy does not record the details of its composition) and refers readers to her note for the entry written on April 29th, one week later (236). Woof rightly perceives a link between the two entries, for it seems that on this later occasion William still had his recently written poem on his mind:

> We . . . went to Johns Grove, sate a while at first. Afterwards William lay, & I lay in the trench under the fence—he with his eyes shut & listening to the waterfalls & the Birds. There was no one waterfall above another—it was a sound of waters in the air—the voice of the air. William heard me breathing & rustling now & then but we both lay still, & unseen by one another—he thought that it would be as sweet thus to lie so in the grave, to hear the *peaceful* sounds of the earth & just to know that ones dear friends were near. (92)

Dorothy's description captures the strange intimacy of William's poem (without ever mentioning it) while also shifting its lyrical stance slightly, since William now seems to imagine the two of them lying "in the grave." For Dorothy's later readers, such a shift might demonstrate the eerily symbiotic nature of their relationship, and in fact earlier editions of the journals have invited this interpretation by reading "ones dear friends" as "*our* dear friends" (emphasis mine). In other words, earlier readers would have believed that the sentence concludes with William imagining the two of them lying together wakefully dead, experiencing the "Peace, peace, peace" of the grave. In her textual analysis of the entry, however, Woof argues that "it is more clearly 'ones' with, as often, no apostrophe," which "emphasizes the solitary, internalized nature of both the present experience (W[illiam] 'with his eyes shut') and the envisaged experience of death." She adds that for William "this was a happy state" (239). It probably was for Dorothy, too, and we might even be able to take that for granted, at least up to a point.[13] What we should not take for granted, however, is the effect Woof's textual emendation has on our sense of William and Dorothy's relationship to death. For example, Elizabeth Fay (who consults Woof's edition of the journals) notes that what "is striking about this entry is that the perceptions are a combination of William's perceiving and Dorothy's imagining of what William is perceiving," but that it is "not a record of her own experience in the 'grave.' It is William's fantasy supported by Dorothy's sympathetic imagination. . . ." (165). Fay's careful analysis reinforces—and builds upon—Woof's findings, situating Dorothy and William on either side of a fantastic graveyard experience. That Dorothy ultimately stops short of the grave—and that William is content to leave her behind—suggests that only poets can tread on such "shadowy ground" (to adapt language from the great "Prospectus" ["Home at Grasmere" 977]). And yet, her "sympathetic imagination" possibly allows her a greater perspective as she moves through but also beyond the subjective—even solipsistic—territories William so clearly enjoyed visiting. We have already seen her trace a similar trajectory in her description of her funeral experience at John Dawson's, and she traces a similar one yet again—but with much greater range—in her narrative of the Greens. Before turning to that quietly powerful account of a community's triumph over personal tragedy, however, I would like to consider Gary Kelly's definition of Romantic death in its broader context in order to clarify Dorothy's relationship to the Grasmerean community she and her brother devoted themselves to so wholeheartedly.

The subject of Kelly's analysis is Felicia Hemans, and he argues that she "was the major British poet of Romantic death, a theme that performed powerful cultural and ideological work in the aftermath of the Revolutionary and Napoleonic crisis of Europe, its empires, and former colonies" (196). He focuses on Hemans' contribution "to the founding of the modern liberal state" through an examination of her post-Revolutionary work, but also points out that

> Romantic death as theme and figure was developed even in the Revolutionary decade of the 1790s, and through the next few decades and beyond it was increasingly set against and in relationship to several other figures. These include natural cataclysms such as storm, flood, and volcanic eruption; biological disasters such as pandemics; and historical catastrophes such as the fall of empires and the disappearance of entire peoples and civilizations into the abyss of oblivion. . . . Romantic death was figured as meaningful death and set against the meaninglessness of mass death, which in turn was widely used to summarize or represent the Revolution and the Napoleonic adventure. (196–97)

Kelly's catalogue seems to take us well beyond Grasmere and John's Grove. His contention, however, that "Romantic death was not a monolithic theme and figure, . . . but rather a field of struggle between varying groups contending to define the sovereign subject and thus the liberal state" (196) reminds us that both Wordsworth and Hemans were published poets working in a public sphere shaped by the events of the French Revolution.[14] Dorothy was of course keenly aware of this sphere—indeed, at times her active involvement in her brother's literary pursuits almost made her a part of it.[15] Nevertheless, in terms of her own writing her relationship to it was finally only tangential, and that was, it seems, her wish, although on two occasions she was encouraged to seek a wider audience for her work. And while her account of her first tour of Scotland in 1803 only just missed being published, it is her first brush with the press in 1808 in relation to her narrative of the Greens that remains perhaps most revealing.[16] " . . . I should detest the idea of setting myself up as an Author." Dorothy's pronouncement, as I point out in my introduction, has profoundly affected our perception of her, making her a perfect foil of Felicia Hemans, who almost literally worked herself to death as she struggled—with a great degree of success—to establish herself as a poet in a male-dominated world.[17] It occurs, however, within her very thoughtful response to the idea of publishing her narrative (raised by her friend Mrs. Clarkson), a response we can now consider more closely.

> My dear Friend I cannot express what pain I feel in refusing to grant any request of yours, and above all one in which dear Mr Clarkson joins so earnestly, but indeed I cannot have that narrative published. My reasons are entirely disconnected with myself, much as I should detest the idea of setting myself up as an Author. I should not object on that score as if it had been an invention of my own it might have been published without a name, and nobody would have thought of me. But on account of the Family of the Greens I cannot consent. Their story was only represented to the world in that narrative which was drawn up for the collecting of the subscription, so far as might tend to produce the end desired, but by publishing this narrative of mine I should bring the children forward to notice as Individuals, and we know not what injurious effect this might have on them. Besides it appears to me that the events are too recent to be published in delicacy to others as well as to the children. . . . Thirty or forty years hence when the Characters of the children are formed and they can be no longer the objects of curiosity, if it should be thought that any service

would be done, it is my present wish that it should then be published whether I am alive or dead. (*Middle Years, 1806–1811* 453–54)

That Dorothy should put the Green children's welfare first is entirely in keeping with everything we know about her, as are of course her gestures of self-effacement. But her letter is also valuable for its depiction of the Grasmere community that is in essence the primary subject of her narrative. Bringing "the children forward to notice as Individuals" would in effect bring them into a public sphere, a point that serves to underscore Grasmere's protective powers. This is not to suggest that the inhabitants of Grasmere necessarily existed in a separate—and by implication "purer"—sphere. Dorothy's concern for the Green children's well-being in relation to the publication of her narrative, however, does sharpen our sense of her relationship to place, and perhaps also clarifies her imaginatively sympathetic response to death. Paradoxically, William's desire to work in a public sphere shaped by revolution (a desire that was inspired to a significant extent by his own trips to France during especially troubled times) influenced his most intimate experiences in Grasmere—or at least, Kelly's findings allow us to perceive this causal link. Implicitly, then, William's fantasy of experiencing a solitary, meaningful death in John's Grove could not really have occurred had he not been actively pursuing a career in poetry. Dorothy's abhorrence of publication, on the other hand, emerges as a reflection of her deep, sympathetic appreciation of the Grasmere community that represented the only public sphere she cared to know. She remains on this side of the grave in order to experience a community's response to death, and it results in her communion with one of its recently departed inhabitants, Sarah Green.

That this communion should occur late in the narrative in a single paragraph that we might be inclined to overlook (or at least subsume in our overall reading experience) even though Dorothy moves inexorably towards it from the very beginning is an illustration of her subtly sophisticated rhetorical practice. Here is the paragraph in its entirety:

Poor Woman! she is now at rest. I have seen one of her Sons playing beside her grave; and all her Children have taken to their new homes, and are chearful and happy. In the night of her anguish if she could but have had a foresight of the kindness that would be shewn to her Children, what a consolation would it have been! With her many cares and fears for her helpless Family she must at that time have mingled some bitter self-reproaches for her boldness in venturing over the Mountains; for they had asked two of the Inhabitants of the Vale to accompany them, who refused to go by that way on account of the bad weather, and she laughed at them for being cowardly. It is now said that her Husband was always fond of doing things that nobody else like to venture upon, though he was not strong and had lost one eye by an accident. She was healthy and active, one of the freshest Women of her years that I ever noticed, and walked with an uncommonly vigorous step. She was forty-five years of age at her Death. (83–84)

In what follows I will attempt to establish the ecological foundations of Dorothy's rhetorical practice as it emerges in her narrative of the Greens as a whole, but especially in relation to her depiction of Sarah Green. I am certainly not the first reader to have shown an interest in Dorothy's identification with her female subject. Susan Levin, for example, suggests that Dorothy "seeks organization and meaning for both the life of the Greens and her own life as she tells her story" (50–51), a claim I do not wish to refute, since it partially inspired my own reading of Dorothy's narrative. But Levin's psychologically oriented analysis of Dorothy's depiction of Sarah Green ultimately relies too heavily on biographical speculation, resulting in a distorted view of both figures.

> The Sarah Green whom Dorothy projects seems to be totally bound up in her children; in dying she commits a mother's greatest crime against a child: total, irrevocable abandonment. Surely Dorothy's feelings about her mother's death work into the narrative. Surely traces of bitterness can be detected in the narrator's attitude towards Sarah, coldly called "the Woman." Dorothy surrounds this statement with qualification but includes it nevertheless: "the Woman had better been at home" [50]. (51)

Dorothy's surrounding "qualification" consists in part of a rhetorical question, which directly follows her seemingly harsh judgement of the "Woman." "[B]ut who shall assert," she continues, "that this same spirit which led her to come at times among her Neighbours as an equal, seeking like them society and pleasure, that this spirit did not assist greatly in preserving her chearful independence of mind through the many hardships and privations of extreme poverty?" (50). Dorothy's question is part of an imaginative process already begun (as we will see) and culminates in the paragraph I have included above. I perceive no traces of bitterness at any point in Dorothy's depiction of Sarah Green, and to what extent that depiction was shaped by memories of her own mother is finally impossible to determine. I suggest, then, that we examine Dorothy's narrative for its more obvious revelations—the fact that Sarah Green was poor, for example. The Greens' "extreme poverty" of course inspired Dorothy to compose her narrative in the first place, which as she explains in her letter to Mrs. Clarkson "was drawn up for the collecting of the subscription" in order to ensure that the orphaned children would not only remain in Grasmere but also receive the best care possible.[18] And in fact this defining attribute of the Greens' condition puts her sympathetic powers of imagination to the test. For as the narrative unfolds it becomes apparent that Dorothy, like other members of her community of a similar social and economic standing, did not really know Sarah Green—indeed, this is one of the central points of her narrative. That Dorothy comes to understand the Greens' life of poverty as a result of telling their story, however, and that she in effect brings a poor woman to life in the act of doing so, is indicative not only of her firm place in the community of Grasmere but also of her understanding of the environmental forces shaping it.

Dorothy's narrative is, as the last part of its title informs us, *Addressed to a Friend*, a fact its first sentence makes clear:

> You remember a single Cottage at the foot of Blentern Gill—it is the only dwelling on the Western Side of the upper reaches of the Vale of Easedale, and close under the mountain; a little stream runs over rocks and stones beside the garden wall, after tumbling down the crags: I am sure you recollect the spot: if not, you remember George and Sarah Green who dwelt there. (43)

This abrupt opening will remind some readers of "Michael," although there are differences between Dorothy's narrative and William's narrative poem. The speaker of "Michael," for example, addresses his readers (whom he imagines to be "youthful Poets" [38]) in the second person and takes them into a "hidden valley" before telling them his story (8), which is to say that he acts as their knowledgeable guide. Dorothy, on the other hand, addresses her narrative to someone familiar with Grasmere (most likely Mrs. Clarkson), which might account for her notably economical approach to storytelling. Except for its opening paragraphs, for example, in which she brilliantly evokes the scene where the tragedy occurred, Dorothy assumes her reader's familiarity with the Grasmerean world of nature the Greens would also have known intimately. This is of course another way of saying that Dorothy's narrative is not especially concerned with natural description, and it poses a challenge for the ecologically oriented reader. After all, James McKusick's definition of "human ecology" as "the study of the complex relationships between human communities and their dwelling places" (70), which is radical for locating nature in human communities, still presupposes the *presence* of those dwelling places, in this case Grasmere and the Lake District. (It might be worth noting that McKusick illustrates his definition through an analysis of "Home at Grasmere.") Dorothy, however, never loses sight of her primary task; she tells a distinctly human story in the hopes of compelling her readers to feel for—and ultimately offer financial support to—the surviving Green children.

But I have already suggested that we can locate the ecology of Dorothy's narrative in her depiction of Sarah Green. Her opening paragraphs describing the Greens being overcome by the forces of nature would seem to be an obvious place to turn for support of such a contention—and indeed I will presently do just that. Paradoxically, however, we cannot appreciate their full ecological significance without also considering Dorothy's morally inflected analysis of Sarah's character, which remains perhaps the most memorable aspect of her narrative.

Dorothy sustains the immediacy of her opening sentence in the paragraphs that follow through an act of the imagination fueled by a knowledge that is local in all senses of the word. Her description of the Greens' last movements, for example, is clearly a reconstruction based on what others in the community had observed (and is a remarkable feat of synthesis when we consider that she began writing her narrative only weeks after the Greens' bodies were found):

> . . . after having spent a few hours at the Sale, they went to the house where the young Woman lived [in order to visit one of their daughters who was in service there], drank tea, and set off homewards at about five o'clock intending to cross over the Fells, and drop down just upon their own Cottage; and they were seen, nearly at the top of the hill in their direct course, by some persons of Langdale, but were never more seen alive. It is supposed that soon afterwards they must have been bewildered by a mist, otherwise they might have reached their own Cottage at the bottom of the hill on the opposite side before daylight was entirely gone. (44)

Details emerge with increasing clarity as Dorothy describes the community's frantic search for the missing couple, until eventually she is led to a spot she herself knows intimately:

> . . . many men went out upon the hills to search; but in vain: no traces of them could be found; nor any tidings heard, except what I

have mentioned, and that a shepherd who had been upon the Mountains on Sunday morning had observed indistinct foot-marks of two Persons who had walked close together. Those foot-marks were now covered with fresh snow: the spot where they had been seen was at the top of Blea Crag above Easedale Tarn, that very spot where I myself had sate down six years ago, unable to see a yard before me, or to go a step further over the Crags. I had left W[illiam] at Stickell Tarn. A mist came on after I had parted with him, and I wandered long, not knowing whither. When at last the mist cleared away I found myself at the edge of the Precipice, and trembled at the Gulph below, which appeared immeasurable. Happily I had some hours of daylight before me, and after a laborious walk I arrived home in the evening. (45–46)

For Susan Wolfson, Dorothy's account of her bewildering experience at the top of Blea Crag is a covertly assertive act; she in effect "writes herself across the Greens' path" (160). Wolfson's argument hinges on the notion that Dorothy's separation from William was the defining moment of her experience, whereas I perceive it as simply part of a causal chain. That such a distinction finally matters, however, will not be apparent until we have internalized the broad outline of Wolfson's argument.

Recalling a separation from William, Dorothy also recalls a world of mist and danger that seems internal as well as external, psychological as well as natural, threatening self-destruction with an intensity hardly dispelled by the matter-of-fact conclusion she applies: 'Happily I had some hours of daylight before me, and after a laborious walk I arrived home in the evening' (pp. 45–46). The Greens' fate was otherwise, but Dorothy's spectral layering of their loss of home and family over her terror away from home and William, once revealed, remains a potential point of reference throughout the course of her narrative, casting a shadowy map of self-interest across the Greens' tragedy and its terms of resolution. (160)

On the simplest level, Wolfson locates a crucial subtext in Dorothy's narrative, one that in some respects parallels Susan Levin's findings. That is to say, both Wolfson and Levin detect a kind of Wordsworthian family drama being enacted just under the narrative's surface. But does this "shadowy map of self-interest" reveal the whole—or even part of the—story? For example, it seems to me that Dorothy's identification, or communion, with Sarah Green intensifies as she proceeds (and in fact begins with her account of her experience on Blea Crag), which if anything reveals a radical *lack* of "self-interest." Because it occurs on an imaginative level, however, the narrative possesses an undercurrent of subjective energy, clearing a path for subtextual interpretation. And yet Dorothy's communion with Sarah Green (the only genuinely psychological event in the narrative) takes place in the shadowless daylight world of Grasmere because the entire community felt the impact of the Greens' deaths. Grasmere's inhabitants gather at their joint funeral in order to pay their respects as well as make sense—collectively—of a tragic event.

The funeral itself, therefore, is perhaps the most important aspect of the narrative's surface, since this is where the living and the dead members of the community finally come together. We are of course now back in (William) Wordsworth territory, and it is in fact probably no accident that Dorothy makes her most Wordsworthian statement just before giving her account of the funeral.[19] "It is, when any unusual event happens," she writes,

> affecting to listen to the fireside talk in our Cottages; you then find how faithfully the inner histories of Families, their lesser and greater cares, their peculiar habits, and ways of life are recorded in the breasts of their Fellow-inhabitants of the Vale; much more faithfully than it is possible that the lives of those, who have moved in higher stations and had numerous Friends in the busy world, can be preserved in remembrance, even when their doings and sufferings have been watched for the express purpose of recording them in written narratives. (53)

In a central chapter of *Wordsworth's Second Nature,* James Chandler rightly perceives a "deprecation of writing in favor of speech" in the poems William began writing shortly after he and Dorothy moved to Grasmere (140).[20] For Chandler, poems such as "The Brothers" and "Michael" reflect his desire to define a "natural culture," or lore (140), and it seems fairly obvious—especially given that the narrative's first sentence distinctly recalls "Michael"— that Dorothy defines and defends this lore all over again in the wake of the Greens' deaths eight years later. Susan Levin also connects Dorothy's statement to William's poetry of 1800, particularly "Michael," in her analysis of the Green narrative; however, I question her dualistic reading of Dorothy's "attempt to write in elements of the people's spoken record" (47). Dorothy "sets up her work," she proceeds to argue, "as a familiar, chatty recounting, personalizing its content, addressing it 'to a Friend'" (47). In other words, Levin perceives these aspects of Dorothy's narrative as rhetorical embellishments, connecting them to her fears that she has not "created a 'faithful'" record" (48), because of course she has created a written account of the Greens' story. I suggest, however, that while Dorothy's narrative certainly acknowledges the superiority of the spoken word it also successfully bridges the gap between spoken and written forms of communication. Indeed, it is her awareness of this division that makes her imaginative communion with Sarah possible.

But as the site for a gathering of the entire community of Grasmere (or at least a representative portion of it), the funeral reveals other divisions as well. Dorothy begins her account of it by informing us that the "pair were buried in one grave on the Friday afternoon," and that a "great number of people of decent and respectable appearance were assembled at the House" (54). The higher and lower orders of Grasmere, then, come together at the Greens' house, and in fact for most, including Dorothy herself, this was the first time they had been—and last time they would be—inside their cottage. Such a contingency affords Dorothy two related "views" of the proceedings. Initially, she simply observes the Greens' extremely modest furnishings. "The furniture of the house," she writes, "was decayed and scanty; but there was one oaken cupboard that was so bright with rubbing that it was plain it had been prized as an ornament and a treasure by the poor Woman then lying in her Coffin" (55). Immediately after this careful blending of sense and sensibility, however (she sees clearly, but with feeling), she records a brief moment of hesitation on her sister-in-law's part that illuminates a crucial aspect of Grasmerean custom, or lore.

> Before the Bodies were taken up a three-penny loaf of bread was dealt out to each of the Guests: Mary was unwilling to take hers, thinking that the Orphans were in no condition to give away anything; she immediately, however, perceived that she ought to accept it, and a Woman, who was near us, observed that it was an ancient custom now much disused; but probably, as the Family had lived long in the Vale, and had done the like at funerals formerly, they thought it proper not to drop the custom on this occasion. (55–56)

In some respects, this moment emerges as perhaps the ideal advertisement for the Wordsworthian perspective in that it locates the survival of rural traditions in the poorest of the poor inhabitants of a well-defined locale. Dorothy herself, it seems, was not aware of this custom (even if she did not hesitate, as her sister-in-law did, in taking a portion of the "three-penny loaf of bread"), and her recording of it ensures that it will remain the property of the "folk" of the Vale. Implicitly, then, she perceives herself as a guardian of tradition, which places her in a superior position to the other members of the community (much like the figure of the poet in relation to his poet-readers at the beginning of "Michael"). And yet, the very fact that she absorbed this new knowledge at the funeral and then chose to disseminate it in writing is a tacit acknowledgement of her dependent status; she realizes that the cultural vitality of Grasmere Vale depends upon its seemingly least powerful inhabitants. Interestingly, had Dorothy not possessed these interrelated points of view she would very likely have left Sarah Green to sleep in the peaceful earth at the funeral's end; instead, she becomes part of her consciousness as a kind of process, like nature itself.

We can now return to the paragraph that in my opinion represents the defining moment of this experience. We recall that it begins with an apostrophe ("Poor Woman!") and that it concludes with a bit of factual information: "She was healthy and active, one of the freshest Women of her years that I ever noticed, and walked with an uncommonly vigorous step. She was forty-five years of age at her Death." Dorothy herself walked with a "vigorous step" (indeed, she records being complimented on her walking "by 2 Cumberland people" in an entry of the Grasmere journals [3]), so obviously she and Sarah had something in common. But that was most likely all they had in common, and in the end this is not what her identification with "the Woman" involves, since we also must acknowledge that her powers of judgment remain firmly intact for the duration of her narrative. Even this close to the end Dorothy still describes Sarah's all-too-human characteristics—her laughing at those who would not take the same path in such dangerous conditions, for example. And yet, even Sarah's flaws are finally subsumed into a kind of pure intellectual space here at the end of the narrative, and in fact it is the presence of this space that best illustrates Dorothy's nascent ecological stance. We of course associate ecology with materiality—and for good reason, since the ecologist must finally base her arguments for a responsible treatment of the earth on physical evidence. With this idea in mind, let us now re-experience Dorothy's communion with her female subject—a communion that at first glance might seem utterly removed from the aims of the ecologist since it occurs on an imaginative level through the use of language:

> In the night of her anguish if she could but have had a foresight of the kindness that would be shewn to her Children, what a consolation would it have been! With her many cares and fears for her helpless Family she must at that time have mingled some bitter self-reproaches for her boldness in venturing over the Mountains. . . . (83)

In imagining the night of Sarah's anguish, Dorothy has fully entered into the life of a woman whose house she had never entered until after she had died, which suggests that her communal experience might simply have come too late. Should Dorothy have made more of an effort to get to know Sarah Green while she was still alive, or did social and economic barriers simply make that impossible? On one level, Dorothy's communion with her female subject at the level of language in a narrative commemorating her death would appear to be a poor substitute for any genuine encounters she could have had with her in life. And yet by capturing this imaginative experience in writing she compels her reader—as well as herself—to re-examine the physical world, that space where human and non-human existence strives for an equilibrium that is perpetually threatened.

Trapped in the Weather of the Days: Dorothy Wordsworth in Her Environment

Commenting on Hyman Eigerman's respectful but also inevitably controversial attempt to locate the poetry in Dorothy Wordsworth's prose through a combination of heavy editing and formal rearrangement that resulted in a release of "burnished imagist poems" (161), Beth Darlington seizes on the essential problem. "[B]y formalizing Dorothy Wordsworth's writing," she argues, "Eigerman denied a significant quality of the journals."

> Unweaving her patterns, he sundered those startling flashes of beauty and insight from the context which entwines them in quotidian experience. Some of our pleasure in reading the journals derives from our surprise at suddenly encountering an arresting moment of vision embedded in a chronicle of ordinary daily motions and from our realization that such moments can be part of the texture of everyday experience. (163)

"Reclaiming Dorothy Wordsworth's Legacy." The title of Darlington's essay beautifully exemplifies its focus on Dorothy's "actual identity and achievements" (162). In considering Dorothy Wordworth's ecology, I have been deeply influenced by Darlington's refreshingly straightforward methodology. That is to say, I accept (as Thomas De Quincey did not) Dorothy's life and work as both sufficient and purposeful, and it is my belief that we still have much to learn from her example.[1] And yet, even Darlington's earnest, clear-sighted approach (which represents a significant moment in the history of scholarship devoted to Dorothy Wordsworth) poses subtle problems for the environmentally oriented reader.

Consider, for example, her intriguing point that part of our pleasure in reading Dorothy's journals comes from our "suddenly encountering an arresting moment of vision embedded in a chronicle of ordinary daily motions." Perhaps the most famous example of such a moment occurs with Dorothy's

arresting description of "[t]he moonshine like herrings in the water," which
I myself have referred to more than once during the course of this work. It
emerges at the end of her brief entry for November 1, 1800:

> W[illiam] & S[toddart] did not rise till 1 o clock. W very sick & very ill.
> S & I drank tea at Lloyds & came home immediately after, a very fine
> moonlight night—The moonshine like herrings in the water. (Grasmere
> journals 30)

Read in its proper context, Dorothy's startling trope swims impressively
into our ken in the wake of perfectly ordinary, even pedestrian, description, which is of course Darlington's point. To put it another way, Darlington does not seek to transfigure Dorothy's work (as Eigerman did), but
rather transform our perception of it by reminding us that Dorothy honed
her perceptual powers while living her life "one day at a time."

But to what extent is a "moment of vision" a *part of* daily life? Darlington's holistic understanding of Dorothy's life and work represents a
kind of environmentalism in the making, but it is compromised by language we tend to associate with her brother as well as certain post-Romantic developments in literature that are the direct result of his influence.[2]
Indeed, Darlington's alternative approach to Dorothy's work might differ
in degree rather than in kind from Eigerman's Modernist procedure—and
not just because of her reliance on diction that we tend to associate with
Virginia Woolf. For in order to prove her basic thesis that "Dorothy Wordsworth's art is her prose," (167) she must ignore her actual poetry (although
in developing her argument she gives an excellent overview of feminist-
oriented critics' sometimes quite negative assessments of Dorothy's poetic
efforts[3]). Of course, nobody is required to read (or like) Dorothy's poetry,
but as I hope the present study has demonstrated, a genuine understanding
of Dorothy Wordsworth's ecology depends on a genuinely holistic approach
to her work. To read her work ecologically, then, is to consider it as a totality—to consider it, that is, as a kind of ecosystem in which even the most
seemingly innocuous elements (such as her children's poems) contribute to
its health and vitality.

But some have doubted the health and vitality of both Dorothy
Wordsworth and her work. For example, Elizabeth Hardwick describes
Dorothy as hopelessly awkward and odd:

> There was always something peculiar about Dorothy Wordsworth;
> she is spoken of as having "wild lights in her eyes," and is remem-

bered as excitable and intense. There is something about her of a Bronte heroine: a romantic loneliness, a sense of having special powers of little use to the world and from which one tries to extract virtue if not self-esteem. She is said to have received several marriage offers, perhaps even from Hazlitt in one of his manic moods. It is hard to imagine any true sympathy between the austere, trembling Dorothy and the Hazlitt who complained that there were no courtesans in Wordsworth's "Excursion." (144)

Dorothy's readers will react as they see fit to this highly imaginative, even De Quincean, portrait; here, I want to examine more closely the relationship Hardwick establishes between (what she perceives to be) Dorothy's rather high-strung personality and the environments that inspired her writing. "Her journals were begun early, spurred on by William," she suggests.

It appears that he realized the need of an "occupation" for Dorothy, an anchor for her free-flying emotions and impressions. The first notes made at Alfoxden in 1798 set the pattern for all of her writing. It is a peculiar one, trapped in the very weather of the days, concentrating upon the bare scenic surface, upon the ineffable and more or less impersonal:

Bright sunshine, went out at 3 o'clock. The sea perfectly calm blue, streaked with deeper colour by the clouds, and tongues or points of sand; on our return a gloomy red. The sun goes down. The crescent moon. Jupiter and Venus. [Alfoxden journal 141]

What rivets the attention in this early journal is not the moon or the mild morning air, but a sudden name. "Walked with Coleridge over the hills," or "walked to Stowey with Coleridge." Even in her youth in the lake region, nature is not a sufficient subject for the whole mind. To name it, to paint it with words is indeed a rare gift. But it is a gift almost dangling in the air. It is the final narrowness of the pictorial, the frustration of the quick microscopic brilliance, unroped by generalization. (145)

Dorothy's extremely limited range of vision has always represented a kind of crux for her readers, but to my knowledge only Hardwick has understood it in such strikingly elemental terms. Indeed, her interpretation of Dorothy's earliest formal journal (which she suggests "set the pattern for all her writing") argues for its author's self-imposed entrapment in the "very weather of the days" of a landscape that rather dubiously fires her "pictorial" imagination. Like De Quincey, then, Hardwick appears dissatisfied with Dorothy's choice of lifestyle—at least in so far as it influenced her as a writer. But while De Quincey shared Dorothy's taste for country living and thus only questioned her lack of professional ambition, Hardwick believes she has discovered its root cause. Her essay is in essence a bemused meditation on a woman who seemed content to live a sadly attenuated life in a series of rural backwaters.[4]

If Hardwick's portrait strikes the environmentally oriented reader as almost a parody of what it means to be a "dweller in the landscape" (to adapt James McKusick's excellent phrase), it nevertheless gestures toward an ecological understanding of Dorothy Wordsworth. But its environmental aspect remains latent, trapped, I would suggest, in the purview of Hardwick's narrowly urban perspective. Conversely, the ecologist is likely to perceive Dorothy's environmental entrapment as the essential condition of her existence, and yet we must also be careful not to interpret this as a simple turning of the tables on Hardwick's anti-rural stance. For as Lawrence Buell has recently posited, "a mature environmental aesthetics—or ethics, or politics— must take into account the inter-penetration of metropolis and outback, of anthropocentric as well as biocentric concerns" (22–23). Interestingly, then, in examining Dorothy Wordsworth's ecology I have theoretically assumed a perspective my subject would have found untenable (since for Dorothy the country and the city remained distinct entities) in order to challenge some of the more biased critical interpretations of her life and work, such as Hardwick's. I would like to stress, however, that I do not profess to have discovered *the* way to read Dorothy Wordsworth; rather, I have tried to perceive her life and work (or at least a representative portion of it) as clearly and straightforwardly as possible. Now, in my view the emergence of Romantic ecology, which represents a significant moment in the development of environmental criticism, has allowed me to do this, and I would like to conclude this examination by considering the benefits of continuing to read her work from an environmental perspective.[5]

In *The Song of the Earth*, Jonathan Bate suggests that John Clare "is among English poetry's subtlest knowers of what the philosopher Edmund Husserl calls 'thing-experience,' *Dingerfahrung*." "Clare's world-horizon," he continues, "was the horizon of the things—the stones, animals, plants, people—that he knew first and knew best. When he went beyond that horizon, he no longer knew what he knew" (153). Bate's assessment of Clare's almost obsessive attachment to place inaugurates a beautifully intimate analysis of

his life and work in relation to some of the key ideas found in French philosopher Gaston Bachelard's phenomenological study, *The Poetics of Space.*

> Bachelard's argument is that we especially love the spaces which afford us
> protection, first those within the house—secret rooms, drawers, chests,
> wardrobes—and then their equivalents in the world, especially nests and
> shells, the respective refuges of vertebrates and invertebrates. Bachelard
> is mesmerized by the interpenetration of indoor and outdoor spaces,
> interior and exterior ecologies. . . . His central theme is what he calls
> *inhabiting,* which is what I call dwelling with the earth. (154–55)

Bate's phenomenological analysis of John Clare (which comprises the bulk of
his sixth chapter, "Nests, Shells, Landmarks") immediately follows his analysis of "Tintern Abbey," which closes his fifth chapter. Readers will recall that
Bate's reading of William's great poem served as an important catalyst for my
own ecological consideration of Dorothy Wordsworth, and in my view he
has fashioned a suggestive interpretive sequence between his fifth and sixth
chapters. In fact, given the respective subject matter of these chapters (the
picturesque and the connections between human and non-human domestic
spaces) I would argue that Dorothy emerges as the (invisible) link uniting
them. My point, however, is not to suggest that Bate *needed* to have con-
sidered how Dorothy bridges the gap between the ecological perspectives of
John Clare and William Wordsworth, for his book is destined to be remem-
bered as a wonderfully inclusive examination of "the poetry of earth."[6] Nevertheless, the very structure of *The Song of the Earth* illustrates that when
it comes to ecological considerations of Romantic-period literature Dorothy Wordsworth remains the "hidden Bird that sang" ("Home at Grasmere"
110).

I have suggested that Dorothy bridges the gap between the ecological
perspectives of John Clare and William Wordsworth, and I believe that
future environmental readings of their works (whether in relation to one
another or not) will help demonstrate this. Including Dorothy in future
considerations of Romantic ecology will also in my view provide us with a
more balanced picture of the period's relationship to later developments in
ecology and environmentalism. For example, we have already encountered
Jonathan Bate's arguments for William Wordsworth's nascent "deep"
ecological stance. James McKusick, however, is even more forthright in his
assessment of John Clare in this regard, stating simply that "Clare's unique
accomplishment in combining a deep sensitivity for natural phenomena with
forceful environmental advocacy clearly entitles him to be regarded as the

first 'deep' ecological writer in the English literary tradition" (78). Perhaps not surprisingly, in according Clare this privileged status McKusick also distances him from the picturesque tradition:

> . . . Clare regards himself as a normal participant in the living world around him, just another inquisitive mammal going about its daily activities. As a result, his poems rarely 'set the scene' in the approved picturesque manner; he provides an accumulation of close-up details rather than sweeping perspectives. (81)

McKusick resembles Bate in his location of the earliest manifestations of a deep ecology in his subject's eschewal of "sweeping perspectives" suggestive of human superiority. And yet in his zeal to merge past and (radical) present perspectives, he reads Clare so deeply that he risks missing the forest for the trees. For while he refers readers to Timothy Brownlow's *John Clare and Picturesque Landscape*, pointing out Clare's "complex response to the tradition of 'picturesque' writing" in the process (238), it seems unlikely that he agrees with Brownlow's assertion that Clare should "be called a 'picturesque' poet" (4). In any event, he does not actually consider this assertion, and because he includes the information related to Brownlow's book in a note it could be said that McKusick has repressed the picturesque in order to remain true to his sense of Clare's "dark-green" language. Turning back to Dorothy Wordsworth, it has been the argument of this book that her ecology cannot be understood properly without also taking into consideration her (not uncomplicated) relationship to the picturesque, which in turn means that she will probably never be thought of as a "deep" ecological writer. Perhaps, then, she should be accepted simply for what she was—a dweller trapped in the weather of the days.

Notes

NOTES TO THE INTRODUCTION

1. Susan Levin provides us with the pertinent bibliographical information: Fragments of the Grasmere journals were first included in the 1851 *Memoirs of William Wordsworth* by Christopher Wordsworth. J. C. Shairp's edition of *Recollections of a Tour Made in Scotland (A.D. 1803)* appeared in 1874, going through three editions by 1894 and even evoking poems from admiring readers. The first extended edition of Dorothy's writing was William Knight's 1897 *Journals of Dorothy Wordsworth* in two volumes; a one-volume edition came out in 1924. (243)

2. I use the terms "ecocriticism" and "environmentalism" (and their variants) interchangeably throughout this book. The terms are not necessarily synonymous, however. See Lawrence Buell's *The Future of Environmental Criticism* ("Preface" viii) for a consideration of the relative merits of each term.

3. Unless otherwise specified, all references in the entire work to either the Alfoxden or Grasmere journals are from *The Grasmere and Alfoxden Journals*, edited by Pamela Woof.

4. Mellor generously paraphrases and also quotes from lines 11 and 1 (respectively) of Dorothy's poem. The text of "Floating Island at Hawkshead" can be found in "Appendix One" of Susan Levin's *Dorothy Wordsworth and Romanticism* (207–08). All references to Dorothy's poetry in the entire work have been taken from Levin's appendix (175–237), which gathers all of Dorothy's (known) extant poems. I discuss "Floating Island at Hawshead" in my third chapter; information related to its possible date of composition will be found there.

5. Pamela Woof's *Dorothy Wordsworth, Writer* (published by the Wordsworth Trust in 1988) and Susan Levin's *Dorothy Wordsworth and Romanticism* (Rutgers, 1987) remain the only separately published monographs on Dorothy Wordsworth. Both are absolutely essential for their insights into Dorothy's work and her relationship with others, especially of course her brother.

I would also single out the following articles, all of which examine on one level or another Dorothy's relationship to genre (I have included dates of publication in parentheses): Rachel Mayer Brownstein, "The Private Life: Dorothy Wordsworth's Journals" (1973); Alec Bond, "Reconsidering Dorothy Wordsworth" (1984, but originally given as a talk at the Wordsworth Conference in England in 1975); Beth Darlington, "Reclaiming Dorothy Wordsworth's Legacy" (1987); Anita Hemphill McCormick, "'I shall be beloved—I want no more': Dorothy Wordsworth's Rhetoric and the Appeal to Feeling in *The Grasmere Journals*" (1990); Kay K. Cook, "Self-Neglect in the Canon: Why Don't We Talk about Romantic Autobiography?" (1990).

6. Dorothy's statement occurs in a letter to Catherine Clarkson (*Middle Years, 1806–1811* 453–54) in which she explains her refusal to publish *A Narrative Concerning George and Sarah Green of the Parish of Grasmere*. I discuss this work in my fourth chapter. References to Dorothy's letters taken from *The Letters of William and Dorothy Wordsworth*, 8 vols., second edition, 1967–1993.

7. In *The Poetry of Dorothy Wordsworth* (1940), Hyman Eigerman presents selections from the journals that he has condensed and arranged in verse form, a gesture at once utterly complimentary and fascinatingly controversial. His transformations should be of interest to any reader of Dorothy Wordsworth.

8. Considering Gittings and Manton's suggestion that Dorothy might have begun her journal after she and her brother had "just heard that they would not be allowed to stay at Alfoxden beyond the early summer of 1798" (Worthen 53), Worthen suggests that the

> immediate cause is more likely to have been the fact that Coleridge had left Nether Stowey on 12 January for at least a fortnight—and perhaps longer—and that, without him and his ever-flowing series of reactions to their everyday experience, both Dorothy and William would have felt a gap in their lives. The journal may well have been started to ensure that they went on seeing, without him, what he always made so memorable: and it would also enable *him* to see what they had been experiencing, when he came back. (53)

Worthen's argument is in keeping with his collectivist approach to biography (*The Gang* is a collectivist biography of Coleridge, the Hutchinsons, and the Wordsworths in 1802, a crucial year for all concerned) and seems plausible. On the other hand, there is nothing to say that Dorothy did not begin her journal in order to capture what they would soon be leaving for their own *and* Coleridge's benefit.

9. Read within the context of the paragraph from which it comes, Johnston's point about Dorothy lack of concern for "public society" might make us a little suspicious of Dorothy's tendencies. "Of the French invasion of Switzerland," he notes further, "which began in late January [when Dorothy

began her journal], and from which William dated his loss of hope in the French cause, she says not a word. . . ." (551). If, however, Dorothy was self-consciously keeping a nature journal, her mentioning of politics might simply have represented an overstepping of generic boundaries. In other words, Dorothy knew what she was doing.

10. Worthen points out that the "ending of the journal exactly corresponded with the breaking up of the winter's period of intense companionship [between Dorothy, William, and Coleridge]. They were now actually *working* together, on *Lyrical Ballads*, where Dorothy did most of the transcription. That was where her writing now went" (57).

11. Gittings and Manton point out that

> the early stages of this Journal show great pains to achieve improvement. . . . Conventional phrases, such as 'mimic of spring' [141], seldom appear later. On the second day (21 January) she tries a piece of fanciful whimsy—'Moss cups more proper than acorns for fairly goblets'[141]—in a manner she never repeats. After these few early uncertainties, her style is assured. (77)

12. The phrase "put herself down" echoes the title of an article published in 1988 by James Holt McGavran Jr., "Dorothy Wordsworth's Journals—Putting Herself Down." McGavran argues that due to her extremely close relationship with her brother Dorothy paid the "terrible price" of "the loss of any firm sense of personal identity" (232). On the broadest level, the present study examines Dorothy's "personal identity," and readers should assume that in the argument that follows I am implicitly responding to McGavran's statement, which obviously parallels Levin's arguments related to Dorothy's "refusals."

13. In some respects, Levin's analysis has its origins in the work of Thomas De Quincey, who in 1839 (that is, after the onset of Dorothy's illness in 1829) came to the following conclusion:

> to me it appears, upon reflection, that it would have been far better had Miss Wordsworth condescended a little to the ordinary mode of pursuing literature; better for her own happiness if she *had* been a blue-stocking: or, at least, if she had been, in good earnest, a writer for the press, with pleasant cares and solicitudes of one who has some little ventures, as it were, on that vast ocean. (204–05).

14. According to Dr. I. I. J. M. Gibson, a Consultant Physician in Geriatric Medicine, and whose advice Gittings and Manton sought regarding Dorothy's health, Dorothy likely "had senile dementia of the type similar to Alzheimer's disease which is genetically determined pre-senile dementia" (282). See the second appendix of Gittings and Manton's biography ("Dorothy Wordsworth's Medical Condition" 282–83) for Dr. Gibson's complete report.

15. Both Levin and Mellor approach Dorothy's work armed with an understanding of a female, "relational self," which Levin points out grows out of "paradigms of female development advanced by such theorists as Nancy

Chodorow [*The Reproduction of Mothering*], Jean Baker Miller [*Toward a New Psychology of Women*], and Carol Gilligan [*In a Different Voice*]" (4). "A drawing together of feminist and psychoanalytical analyses," she proceeds, "provides a further way of understanding what Gilligan would term Dorothy Wordsworth's 'different voice'" (4–5). It should be pointed our, however, that in her analysis of Dorothy's Grasmere journals Mellor first refers to the work of Margaret Homans [*Women Writers and Poetic Identity: Dorothy Wordsworth, Emily Bronte, and Emily Dickinson*], James Holt MacGavran Jr., and Susan Levin before asking why Dorothy's self has "so often been read as either repressed or inadequate, her writing defined as the failure to achieve narrative representation of a distinct subjectivity?" (144). Mellor's analysis, then, like my own, offers an alternative view of Dorothy's self.

16. See James McKusick's *Green Writing: Romanticism and Ecology*, especially 15–16, for a lucid account of the origins of Romantic ecology. *Romantic Ecology* is the title of Jonathan Bate's seminal study of William Wordsworth and the environmental tradition (published in 1991), and McKusick has it—as well as the work of Karl Kroeber—specifically in mind when he notes that "[m]uch of the squabbling between New Historicists and Ecocritics has been carried on in deplorably simplistic and even *ad hominem* terms. To the extent that there is a serious issue at stake, it centers around the question of whether Nature 'really exists' or is merely a construct of social and political history" (15).

17. The following critique of Bate's interpretation of William's poem has its origins in a course I taught in the spring semester of 2005 at the University of Calgary. I titled the course "Romantic Ecology," and it revolved around a consideration of four Romantic figures: Dorothy and William Wordsworth, Samuel Taylor Coleridge, and John Clare. In one class in particular we examined closely the fifth chapter of Bate's *The Song of the Earth*, "The Picturesque Environment," from which my quotations come. I would like to acknowledge the contributions of the following students for helping me shape my argument: Alicia Baudais, Jennifer Campbell, Anna Cotton, David Fletcher, Katherine Fletcher, Patty Gonzalez, Rachel Herbert, Kirsten Inglis, Chris Jordan, Jennifer Leslie, Jennifer Lobay, Carly Nicholson, Colin Schulhauser, Jeremy Sexsmith, Amy Shoup, and Stephanie Wong.

18. Unless otherwise specified, all references in the entire work to William's poetry have been taken from Stephen Gill's *William Wordsworth* (in the Oxford Authors Series). Gill's edition includes the 1805 version of *The Prelude*. Numbers in parentheses refer to line numbers.

19. *The Song of the Earth* was published in 2000, nearly ten years after *Romantic Ecology*. Kroeber's *Ecological Literary Criticism: Romantic Imagining and the Biology of Mind* was published in 1994, James McKusick's *Green Writing* in 2000. A perusal of all four books' indexes will reveal the scant attention

Dorothy receives. Onno Oerlemans' *Romanticism and the Materiality of Nature* (2002) represents a recent exception as it contains a chapter on travel writing that includes a close reading of Dorothy's *Recollections of a Tour Made in Scotland*. I consider Oerleman's work on Dorothy in my second chapter.

20. The frequency of the moon's appearance in the Alfoxden journal is possibly another indicator of its experimental status, Dorothy delighting in describing its various appearances and phases as well as the changes it wrought on the landscapes she so regularly moves through. It might be worth noting that William's "A Night-Piece" represents a poetic transformation of an entry from a week before (January 25, 1798). Interestingly, the moon is the focal point of William's poem, eclipsing Dorothy's other concerns in the passage. See Johnston's *The Hidden Wordsworth* (551–53) for an excellent consideration of both William's poem and Dorothy's journal entry.

21. These changes would include, of course a growing industrialism, but there was also a desire for improvement in general in the eighteenth century. For a discussion of the relationship between "improving" conditions and the emergence of ecology, see Donald Worster's *Nature's Economy: A History of Ecological Ideas*, 3–25. Worster's discussion revolves around Gilbert White, a figure not unlike Dorothy in his interest in describing natural scenes rather than his "interior self" (5).

NOTES TO CHAPTER ONE

1. Jonathan Wordsworth's statement appears in his influential article, "On Man, on Nature, and on Human Life." For a brief but excellent overview of the central issues surrounding the composition of "Home at Grasmere" (as well as a partial rebuttal of Jonathan Wordsworth's claims) see Kenneth R. Johnston's *Wordsworth and* The Recluse, 370 (note 10).

2. In "'Home at Grasmere': Ecological Holiness," Kroeber argues that, "[f]rom its first lines the poem demonstrates how awareness of time liberates man from the prison of immediacy. . . . This liberation entails no escape to some other, more idealized realm of being. Consciousness of time is alertness to the *continuity* of actual existence" (133). In a sense, Kroeber hints that arguments about the composition of the poem might not be as important as the poem's actual treatment of time. On the other hand, William's very treatment of time might in fact suggest a process of mystification (through an erasure of temporal borders), in which case arguments concerning the composition of the poem take precedence once again.

3. See, for example, Alec Bond's "Reconsidering Dorothy Wordsworth," which describes the Grasmere journals as "a piece of writing which contains an almost submerged but tightly unifying dramatic thread" (206), the "thread"

of course being the relationship between brother and sister that the journals so carefully if also at times unconsciously trace.

4. In her introduction to her edition of Dorothy's journals, Pamela Woof reminds us that "[t]he writing, even during these early years of comparative space, had to be fitted into corners of the day" (xviii).

5. See Carl Ketcham's "Dorothy Wordsworth's Journals, 1824–1835" for fascinating proof of this.

6. The classic examination of Dorothy's interest in the picturesque (published in 1964) remains John Nabholtz's "Dorothy Wordsworth and the Picturesque."

7. For a challenging exploration of the relationship between human beings and the landscape in eighteenth and nineteenth-century painting, see John Barrell's *The Dark Side of the Landscape: the Rural Poor in English Painting, 1730—1840*. His chapter on John Constable (131–64) is especially pertinent in this context.

8. For a fascinating discussion of weather and literature (surprisingly, a seldom-discussed subject), see Jonathan Bate's chapter in *The Song of the Earth* entitled "Major Weather" (94–118). His discussion of Keats's "To Autumn" (102–10) is especially illuminating.

9. Naomi Schor's *Reading in Detail: Aesthetics and the Feminine* allows us to read Dorothy's penchant for detail in a broader, feminist context.

10. Arnold published his famous introductory essay (for an edition of William's poetry published in the Golden Treasury series) in 1879, and, as A. Dwight Culler points out, "[i]t largely determined the view of Wordsworth for many decades" (574). For text and commentary see *Poetry and Criticism of Matthew Arnold*, edited by Culler.

NOTES TO CHAPTER TWO

1. See James Buzard's *The Beaten Track*, especially pages 1–2 (for information on the *OED*'s entry on "tourist") and pages 18–20 (for commentary on "The Brothers").

2. In her introduction to a recent edition of the *Recollections*, Carol Kyros Walker points out that when it was completed "its style betrayed remarkable coherence, with a concern for ordering the entire work and providing it with a unity that would be both pleasing to and convenient for the reader" (Walker 18). All references to the *Recollections* are from de Selincourt's standard edition of Dorothy's journals (in two volumes), Volume I.

3. In my chapter on the Grasmere journals, I suggest that Dorothy's memory worked centrifugally, which points to a possible contradiction in terms. I am referring in this instance, however, to what Dorothy desired most, which was clearly a home. Thus, the idea of having a home nourished Dorothy's imagination. It centred her existence.

4. In my chapter on the Grasmere journals, I argue that the four separate journals Dorothy kept between May of 1800 and January of 1803 accrete to form an ecosystem. It seems that we cannot make exactly the same claim for the *Recollections*, particularly since Dorothy herself was careful to distinguish her travel narrative from her previous (journal) work. (And in this context it is interesting to note that while Dorothy was careful to title her travel narrative, she did not feel compelled to title her most famous writings, perhaps because she felt confident that they were simply an extension of her day-to-day life in Grasmere. What we should come to call them, then, was self-evident.) Nevertheless, her decision to simulate a journal approach ultimately transforms the nature of the work itself. It behaves like a journal, and therefore I think we can perceive Dorothy's most famous travel narrative as an ecosystem, even if this is not my first order of business here.

5. See the second chapter of Lawrence Buell's *The Future of Environmental Criticism* ("The World, the Text, and the Ecocritic" 29–61) for a timely discussion of "the disparate ways that literary texts evoke and particularize fictive environmentality" (30). See also *The Greening of Literary Scholarship: Literature, Theory, and the Environment*, edited by Steven Rosendale, for an investigation (from a variety of perspectives) of issues related to ecocriticism. Rosendale's introduction ("Extending Ecocriticism") is particularly interesting for the light it sheds on some of our more ingrained notions about "environmental" texts.

6. See the final section (entitled "Cosmic Ecology: the Growing Plant" [216–24]) of M. H. Abrams' essay "Coleridge and the Romantic Vision of the World" for evidence of Coleridge's proto-ecological sensibility. James McKusick pointed me the way to Abrams' excellent study of Coleridge.

7. See Levin's discussion in which she concentrates on the "moist, dripping, hidden cave . . . [as] an image easily associated with femininity" (80). Elizabeth Bohls also refers to this scene, albeit from a slightly different perspective: "[The] *Recollections'* disruption of picturesque repose [and for Bohls, Dorothy's description of the Highland hut represents one of these disruptions] points to a suppressed anxiety on the woman tourist's part, a sense of her own suspect credentials" (199). Bohls's discussion ("Dorothy Wordsworth and the cultural politics of scenic tourism" [170–208]) is especially illuminating for its treatment of Dorothy's travel writing in relation to women's negotiations of the masculine aesthetic categories that came into being in the eighteenth century and which ultimately influenced texts such as the *Recollections*.

8. "The Birches on the Crags beautiful, Red brown & glittering—the ashes glittering spears with their upright stems. . . ." (48).

9. See Robert Mellin's "Dorothy Wordsworth, Ecology, and the Picturesque" for an environmentally oriented discussion of the Alfoxden journal.

10. For example, Dorothy's distaste for Glasgow emerges quite clearly in the *Recollections*: "Saw nothing remarkable after leaving Bothwell, except the first view of Glasgow, at some miles distance, terminated by the mountains of Loch Lomond. The suburbs of Glasgow extend very far, houses on each side of the highway,—all ugly, and the inhabitants dirty" (235). And yet, in her description of the Highland hut Dorothy takes pleasure in imagining the "London pantomime-maker" and Drury Lane. Like most of us, then, Dorothy's reactions to her surroundings were not simple, but richly multifarious.

11. Coleridge's letter was written in early November of 1799, on or around November 10th. For text of his letter, see the *Collected Letters of Samuel Taylor Coleridge*, Vol. I, page 545.

NOTES TO CHAPTER THREE

1. I have used the last four lines of Gary Snyder's thought-provoking poem as the epigraph for this chapter because I believe that they capture the essential spirit of Dorothy Wordsworth's poetry. Taken as a whole, however, Snyder's poem might sit uneasily beside Dorothy's decidedly less intense work. I include Snyder's poem here, then, in its entirety so that readers can decide for themselves.

   For/From Lew
   Lew Welch just turned up one day,
   live as you and me. "Damn, Lew" I said,
   "you didn't shoot yourself after all."
   "Yes I did" he said,
   and even then I felt the tingling down my back.
   "Yes you did, too" I said—"I can feel it now."
   "Yeah" he said,
   "There's a basic fear between your world and
   mine. I don't know why.
   What I came to say was,
   teach the children about the cycles.
   The life cycles. All the other cycles.
   That's what it's all about, and it's all forgot." (*Axe Handles* 7)

2. William published three of Dorothy's poems in his 1815 *Poems*, including "An address to a Child in a high wind," where it was published as "Address to a Child, During a boisterous Winter Evening." As previously noted, texts (including variations) of Dorothy's poems can be found in Levin (175–237).

3. Dorothy mentions the day before that William had composed "part of" this poem (79).

4. The prosodist notices that the lines Dorothy recites could comprise the middle portion of a stanza from William's poem (that is, lines 2–4), since *Peter Bell's* five-line stanza rhymes abccb. Similarly, Wordsworth cast his poem in iambic tetrameter (allowing for substitutions of course), which accords with the lines Dorothy (ostensibly) quotes. It might be worth noting, however, that "The Emigrant Mother" is itself cast in iambic tetrameter, and even possesses a similar rhyme scheme (in its use of internal couplets).

5. She points out, however, that Dorothy did try and compose verses the next day, thus linking this entry with the one that follows it. Woof's note for the entry of March 17th can be found on pages 227–28 of her edition of Dorothy's journals.

6. In a sense, Thomas De Quincey set the discussion in motion in his (perfectly De Quincean) analysis of Dorothy's personality, which, significantly perhaps, he intersperses in his rambling and revealing piece on William. (See his essay entitled "Wordsworth" in his *Recollections of the Lakes and the Lake Poets*, especially pages 131–33 and 197–205.) Margaret Homans' *Women Writers and Poetic Identity* (1980), however, remains perhaps the best introduction to twentieth-century, feminist-oriented considerations of Dorothy's identity as a poet. Homans considers how three nineteenth-century women poets (Dorothy Wordsworth, Emily Bronte, and Emily Dickinson) "attempt to shape for themselves their own identities as poets in response to a literary tradition that depends on and reinforces the masculine orientation of language and the poet" (3). Critics of Dorothy's poetry have been responding to Homans' assertions (favourably, but also with varying degrees of skepticism) ever since her book appeared. (Homans herself partially replied—as well as demonstrated her debt—to her critics with her 1986 publication, *Bearing the Word: Language and Female Experience in Nineteen-Century Women's Writing*, which contains a substantial chapter on Dorothy's poetry, "Building Refuges: Dorothy Wordsworth's Poetics of the Image.") See Susan Wolfson's "Dorothy Wordsworth in Conversation with William" for a convenient adumbration (through the 1980's) of twentieth-century work on the subject. Recently, Elizabeth Fay has put forth the tantalizing notion that William Wordsworth "the poet, as opposed to the man, is more than William Wordsworth and more than 'a man speaking to men.' He is at once a performance of himself and two enacting selves: William and Dorothy Wordsworth combined" (3). The subject of Dorothy's poetic relationship to William (and vice-versa) is far from exhausted!

7. Levin considers "To my Niece Dorothy, a sleepless Baby" to be Dorothy's earliest poem, speculating that it was composed some time in 1805. She discusses the difficulties involved in establishing dates of composition for Dorothy's poems (see pages 175–76 of her appendix), and in all instances I have been guided by her meticulously researched conjectures.

8. See Abrams' classic essay "The Correspondent Breeze: A Romantic Metaphor" (first published in 1957) where he examines the aeolian qualities of such poems as *The Prelude*, "The Aeolian Harp," and "Ode to the West Wind," working towards a generic categorization of these poems in the process. His equally influential essay "Structure and Style in the Greater Romantic Ode" might also be pertinent in relation to my analysis. In general, Abrams' work illuminates for us the kind of poetry Dorothy did *not* write. Both essays have been conveniently collected in *The Correspondent Breeze*.

9. See William's Preface to *Lyrical Ballads* (600) for his discussion of his avoidance of personification in his poems. I believe we tend to simplify Wordsworth's attitude towards the trope, perhaps in much the same way some have simplified Ruskin's definition of *pathetic fallacy*. For example, in a recently published dictionary of prosody (*The Poet's Dictionary*), William Packard defines pathetic fallacy as personification taken to a kind of ridiculous extreme, which is ultimately a distortion of Ruskin's sense of the device. (See pages 62–76 of *The Literary Criticism of John Ruskin* [edited by Harold Bloom] for Ruskin's definition—and extended consideration—of pathetic fallacy. His definition originally appeared in Volume III of *Modern Painters*, published in 1856.) Of course, personification and pathetic fallacy are similar in their anthropomorphic rendering of the world and its phenomena. Ecologically oriented literary scholars are also, however, beginning to rethink these traditionally maligned devices, perceiving their anthropomorphism as vital to an ecological understanding of the world. See Helena Feder's fascinating "Ecocriticism, New Historicism, and Romantic Apostrophe" for a more detailed discussion of the links between ecology and anthropomorphism.

10. Which is to say we should be on our guard against reading the poem as a duality. The legacy of Cartesian thinking and its relationship to environmental disaster forms an important subtext of Jonathan Bate's *The Song of the Earth*. "The major philosophical revolutions since the seventeenth century," he writes [and he specifically has Descartes as well as Bacon in mind here], "have constituted a progressive severance of humankind from nature that has licensed, or at least neglected, technology's ravaging of the earth's finite resources" (245).

11. Worster points out that Paul Sears has called the field of ecology, "'a subversive subject.' With remarkable suddenness it has mounted a powerful threat to established assumptions in society and in economics, religion, and the humanities, as well as other sciences and their ways of doing business" (23).

12. "The dating of . . . ['Grasmere—A Fragment'] is uncertain," Susan Levin notes,

> although its position in the Coleorton Commonplace Book indicates an early composition. [William] Knight prints a version of the long

poem with this epigraph: 'This is extracted from a copy of an appendix to *Recollections of a Tour in Scotland* by Dorothy Wordsworth, written by Mrs. Clarkson, September-November 1805. It was composed by the poet's sister. In February 1892 it was published in *The Monthly Packet* under the title "Grasmere: A Fragment," and with the signature "Rydal Mount, September 26, 1829." It is now printed from the MS. of 1805.—Ed.' (187)

13. "The afternoon was not chearful but it did not rain until we came near Windermere. I am always glad to see Stavely it is a place I dearly love to think of—the first mountain village that I came to with Wm when we first began our pilgrimage together" (The Grasmere journals 131–32).

14. Perhaps no one has explored (both implicitly and explicitly) Burke's categories in relation to masculine and feminine Romanticism as thoroughly as Anne K. Mellor has. She does not actually discuss "Grasmere—A Fragment," but her interpretation of "Floating Island at Hawkshead" (in a chapter devoted to an examination of Romantic modes of self-presentation via a comparison/contrast of William and Dorothy's work) is exemplary. See *Romanticism and Gender*, 144–69.

15. "[William] Wordsworth may well be regarded as one of the first inventors of 'human ecology,' if by that phrase we mean the study of the complex relationships between human communities and their dwelling places. The fullest exemplification of Wordsworth's concept of human ecology occurs in the poem 'Home at Grasmere.' . . ." (*Green Writing* 70). See pages 70–73 of McKusick's work for an ecological reading of William's poem.

16. And shouldn't we at least entertain the idea that Dorothy might have framed the last line of her poem while thinking of both "I Wandered Lonely as a Cloud" and the journal entry that inspired William's poem in the first place? And if this were so, wouldn't this potentially inspire a different analysis from Levin?

17. See *The Academic Postmodern and the Rule of Literature*, especially its sixth chapter, "Romanticism and Localism" (135–59). Using "Tintern Abbey" as his example, Simpson argues that

> [i]t is in this pure, abstract spot of time, between recollection ('recognitions dim and faint') and projection ('for future years'), that Wordsworth reveals himself to be *nowhere*. The best-known and best-loved of all romantic poets of place is, after close inspection, written as constantly out of place. (155)

18. *Natural Supernaturalism*, 276.

19. James McKusick's reflections on Coleridge might be relevant in this context when he points out that Coleridge's "turn to a more conservative and essentially Burkean political views (in such late works as *On the Constitution of Church and State*) remains compatible with an organic conception of social organization." This is because

he envisions an evolving and (ideally) self-regulating relationship between individual members of the "clerisy" and the established institutions of church and state. Coleridge's commitment to an organic model of human society may be regarded as a constant element that underpins the shifting and often inconsistent expression of his political views during the course of his intellectual career. (41)

20. See Chapter One.

21. Our appearance in the poem sets a second narrative into motion—at least potentially. It would also be a beautifully ironic narrative, since in the course of our wanderings we would discover that the "Isle is passed away." There would, then, be nothing for us to see. Is Dorothy here perhaps subtly parodying the picturesque? The poem contains many ocular references (and notice that our "eyes" instead of our bodies will do the turning while we are out wandering), but it is finally most concerned with process, the ecological life of things that exists beyond the vanishing point of a picturesque aesthetic.

NOTES TO CHAPTER FOUR

1. References to the *Essays on Epitaphs* are from *William Wordsworth: Selected Prose*, edited by John O. Hayden.

2. Caught in an early-spring snowstorm, they fell over a precipice at the top of Blea Crag. "It was a month yesterday since the sad event happened" (61), Dorothy writes in her narrative account. All references to the Green narrative are from de Selincourt's edition (referred to parenthetically as *A Narrative* where necessary), which was first published in 1936.

3. Quotation from the "Argument" which precedes Book V of *The Excusion*, *The Poetical Works of William Wordsworth*, Volume 5. William introduces the character of the Priest at this point in his poem.

4. The editor of the *Essays upon Epitaphs* notes that the "first essay was not only printed in *The Friend* but also appeared as a note to *The Excursion*, Books Five, Six, and Seven of which were written at about the same time and share thoughts and even occasional phrasing with the essay" (322). Johnston points out that the "manuscript history of Books V-IX is so tangled that it may never be known exactly" (285).

5. William gave the details of the poem's composition in the letter to Coleridge in which it appeared. "[I]n passing through the churchyard I stopped at the grave of the poor Sufferers," he writes, "and immediately afterwards composed the following stanzas; *composed* I have said, I ought rather to have said effused, for it is the mere pouring out of my own feeling. . . ." (*Middle Years, 1806–1811* 219). William's correction points to the poem's spontaneous creation, which in turn suggests his slight opinion of it.

It should be noted that Levin refers to the version of the poem De Quincey included in his "Recollections of Grasmere," not the longer poem William originally included in his letter to Coleridge ("copied into the letter by D. W.," as the editors point out [*Middle Years, 1806–1811* 219]). That version, which he titled "Elegiac Stanzas composed in the Churchyard of Grasmere," contains five more stanzas than the one De Quincey published. William did not publish either version of the poem, another indication of his negative opinion of it. For texts of the respective poems, see De Quincey's *Recollections of the Lakes and the Lake Poets* (268–69) and *Letters* (*Middle Years, 1806–1811* 219–20).

6. The word "unknown," we recall, occurs in the narrative section of "Grasmere—A Fragment": "A Stranger, Grasmere, in thy Vale, / All faces then to me unknown" (49–50).

7. In his discussion of William Gilpin's relationship the picturesque in *The Song of the Earth*, Jonathan Bate notes that "[f]or picturesque tourists . . . impressive new industrial sites were objects of admiration just as much as ancient ruins and imposing cliffs" (143). Dorothy was of course familiar with Gilpin's work, and here she adopts something of a middle position, impressed with one example of industry, disgusted with another.

8. Clare's remarkable poem (which he appears to have written in 1831) can be found in Jonathan Bate's well-chosen collection, *"I Am": the Selected Poetry of John Clare* (141–43).

9. In her note for the entry, Woof points out that Shacklock was "a pauper, mother of a 'baseborn daughter' Betty, born 1768, buried 1796, a pauper" (182).

10. Dorothy begins the entry by noting that "Coleridge Wm & John went from home to go upon Helvellyn with Mr Simpson" (20). It could be said, then, that Dorothy was content to let the men experience a more traditional form of the sublime (that is, they climb a mountain) while she ended up in a churchyard communing with a dead woman, a different but no less intense form of the sublime, perhaps.

11. See Gill, *A Life* (266–67), for a succinct review of the reviews of *Poems, in Two Volumes*.

12. See Curtis' headnote to his printed version of the poem for a consideration of the poem's structural oddities (*Wordsworth's Experiments* 176). I have quoted from Gill's printed version of the poem, which regularizes punctuation.

13. It was definitely not a happy state for Coleridge, however. In her note for Dorothy's entry, Woof points out that for Coleridge "the notion of lying awake in the grave was 'frightful' (*Biographia Literaria* xxii [141]). . . ." (239–40). Interestingly, Coleridge's response had its origins in some lines William had intended for his "Intimations" Ode (which he had of course begun at this time). Woof transcribes the lines in which he speculates that

for the child "the grave / Is but a lonely bed without the sense or sight / Of day or the warm light, / A place of thought where we in waiting lie" (239), and also notes that William subsequently removed them from his poem. These lines indicate, however, just how peculiarly focused his thoughts on death were at this time.

14. I do not wish to simplify Kelly's argument, however, which has a distinctly gendered edge. Indeed, he points out that Hemans's success as a female poet was paradoxical, since

> . . . on the one hand Hemans's wide readership and particularized recognition, like that accorded other women writers working in the same vein, could be argued to have contributed to the founding of the modern liberal state by representing and disseminating widely the model of subjectivity on which the state depended. On the other hand, this influence did not result in women being accorded the same sovereign subjectivity, the same capacity to represent themselves, in culture, society, or the processes of the modern liberal state, including suffrage. (196–97)

15. Dorothy's method of expressing herself in the Grasmere journals sometimes makes it difficult to distinguish authorship. In October of 1800, for example, William was hard at work on what became the "Preface" to *Lyrical Ballads*, and on October 5 she records that "Wm and I were employed all the morning in writing an addition to the preface" (24). Did Dorothy, then, actually contribute to the document we associate most with the origins of the Romantic "movement"? Considering how much time William spent discussing his ideas with her (on October she records that "he talked much about the object of his Essay for the 2nd volume of LB" [23]), it is pleasant to think so.

16. See Carol Kyros Walker's introduction to the Yale edition of *Recollections of a Tour Made in Scotland* (23–24) for her account of Dorothy's interactions with those interested in publishing her work. It seems that she "accepted the idea of publication on practical grounds," since it "would bring in some money for further travel abroad," but that apparently Samuel Rogers (the poet and friend of the Wordsworths) "was not successful in locating a publisher or working out an arrangement through a bookseller" (24).

17. The Wordsworth family did in fact meet Hemans, who was a passionate admirer of William's poetry. But while Duncan Wu speculates that the "two writers evidently got on" during her visit to the Lake District in 1830, using as evidence the stanza in "Extempore Effusion on the Death of James Hogg" (composed in 1835) in which William praises her (491), Juliet Barker tells a different story. Writing to the Wordsworths' son-in-law Edward Quillinan, Sara Hutchinson reported that "[f]or one *long* fortnight we had Mrs Hemans & one of her boys," while William himself

described her in a letter to George Huntly Gordon as a "great Enthusiast both in Poetry and music" before adding with an ironic edge that she "enjoys this beautiful Country as much as any one can do who is new to such scenery" (qtd. in Barker 622–23). We do not have Dorothy's reactions to Hemans's visit, although in 1828 she speculated that she "must be a sweet-minded woman" (Hill 175).

18. The decision to raise money by subscription was preventative, as Dorothy explains:

   From the moment we heard that their Parents were lost we anxiously framed plans for raising a sum of money for the purpose of assisting the Parish in placing them with respectable Families; and to give them a little school-learning; and I am happy to tell you that others, at the same time, were employing their thoughts in like manner; and our united efforts have been more successful than we had dared to hope. (61)

19. It might be worth reminding ourselves at this point that the narrative, as its headnote informs us, "was drawn up by Dorothy Wordsworth at the request of her Brother, William Wordsworth," and that "he entreated that she would give a *minute detail* of all the particulars which had come within her notice" (41).

20. See Chandler's sixth chapter, "Natural Lore" (130–55).

NOTES TO THE CONCLUSION

1. I have already quoted a portion of De Quincey's psychological assessment of Dorothy (see the introduction, note 13). I refer to De Quincey again here because Darlington's argument in part grows out of her consideration—and eventual refutation—of his views.

2. In the eighth chapter of *Natural Supernaturalism* ("The Poet's Vision: Romantic and Post-Romantic"), M. H. Abrams considers Romanticism's pervasive influence on modern literature. "[T]he moment of consciousness, the abrupt illumination in an arrest of time," he argues, "has become a familiar component in modern fiction, where it sometimes functions, like Wordsworth's spots of time, as a principle of literary ogranization, by signalizing the essential discoveries or precipitating the narrative resolution" (419). In particular, see pages 418–27 ("Varieties of the Modern Moment").

3. See pages 165–66 of Darlington's essay for her particularly cogent critique of Margaret Homans' *Women Writers and Poetic Identity*.

4. Hardwick's urban bias emerges almost from the very beginning of her essay: "[I]t was forever narrowing, confining, and defining," she writes, "but the country seemed to represent Dorothy's undeviating inclination even more than William's" (143).

5. See the introduction of Buell's *The Future of Environmental Criticism* ("The Emergence of Environmental Criticism" [1–28]) for a multifaceted discussion of the relationship between Romantic criticism and the "environmental turn in literary and cultural studies" (1).

6. The phrase of course opens Keats's "On the Grasshopper and the Cricket." It also serves as one of the epigraphs for Bate's book.

Bibliography

Abrams, M. H. "Coleridge and the Romantic Vision of the World." *The Correspondent Breeze: Essays on English Romanticism.* New York: Norton, 1984. 192–224.

———. *Natural Supernaturalism.* New York: Norton, 1971.

———. "Structure and Style in the Greater Romantic Lyric." *The Correspondent Breeze: Essays on English Romanticism.* New York: Norton, 1984. 76–108.

———. "The Correspondent Breeze: A Romantic Metaphor." *The Correspondent Breeze: Essays on English Romanticism.* New York: Norton, 1984. 25–43.

Barker, Juliet. *Wordsworth: a Life.* London: Penguin, 2000.

Barrell, John. *The Dark Side of the Landscape: the Rural Poor in English Painting, 1730–1840.* Cambridge: Cambridge UP, 1980.

Bate, Jonathan. *Romantic Ecology: Wordsworth and the Environmental Tradition.* London: Routledge, 1991.

———. *The Song of the Earth.* Cambridge: Harvard UP, 2000.

Bohls, Elizabeth. *Women Travel Writers and the Language of Aesthetics, 1716–1818.* New York: Cambridge UP, 1995.

Bond, Alec. "Reconsidering Dorothy Wordsworth." *Charles Lamb Society Bulletin* (July-October 1984): 194–207.

Brownlow, Timothy. *John Clare and Picturesque Landscape.* Oxford: Oxford UP, 1983.

Brownstein, Rachel Mayer. "The Private Life: Dorothy Wordsworth's Journals." *Modern Language Quarterly* 34 (1973): 48–63.

Buell, Lawrence. *The Future of Environmental Criticism: Environmental Crisis and Literary Imagination.* Oxford: Blackwell, 2005.

Buzard, James. *The Beaten Track: European Tourism, Literature, and the Ways to Culture: 1800–1919.* New York: Oxford UP, 1993.

Chandler, James. *Wordsworth's Second Nature: a Study of the Poetry and Politics.* Chicago: U of Chicago P, 1984.

Chodorow, Nancy. *The Reproduction of Mothering.* Berkeley: U of California P, 1978.

Clare, John. *"I Am": the Selected Poetry of John Clare.* Ed. Jonathan Bate. New York: Farrar, Straus, and Giroux, 2003.

Coleridge, Samuel Taylor. *Biographia Literaria*. James Engell and W. Jackson Bate, eds. The Collected Works of Samuel Taylor Coleridge 7. Princeton: Bollingen Series LXXV, Princeton UP, 1983.

———. *Collected Letters of Samuel Taylor Coleridge*. Ed. E. L. Griggs. 6 vols. London: Oxford UP, 1956–71.

Cook, Kay K. "Self Neglect in the Canon: Why Don't We Talk about Romantic Autobiography?" *Auto/Biography Studies* 5 (1990): 88–98.

Culler, A. Dwight, ed. *Poetry and Criticism of Matthew Arnold*. Boston: Houghton Mifflin, 1961.

Curtis, Jared R. *Wordsworth's Experiments with Tradition: the Lyric Poems of 1802*. Ithaca: Cornell UP, 1971.

Darbishire, Helen, ed. *Journals*. Oxford: Oxford UP, 1958.

Darlington, Beth. "Reclaiming Dorothy Wordsworth's Legacy." *The Age of William Wordsworth: Critical Essays on the Romantic Tradition*. Eds. Kenneth R. Johnston and Gene Ruoff. New Brunswick: Rutgers UP, 1987. 160–72.

Davies, Hunter. *William Wordsworth: a Biography*. New York: Atheneum, 1980.

Davis, Robert Con. "The Structure of the Picturesque: Dorothy Wordsworth's Journals." *The Wordsworth Circle* 9 (1978): 45–49.

De Quincey, Thomas. *Recollections of the Lakes and the Lake Poets*. New York: Penguin, 1986.

Eigerman, Hyman. *The Poetry of Dorothy Wordsworth*. New York: Columbia UP, 1940.

Fadem, Richard. "Dorothy Wordsworth: A View from 'Tintern Abbey.'" *The Wordsworth Circle* 9 (1978): 17–32.

Fay, Elizabeth A. *Becoming Wordsworthian: A Performative Aesthetic*. Amherst: U of Massachusetts P, 1995.

Feder, Helen. "Ecocriticism, New Historicism, and Romantic Apostrophe." *The Greening of Literary Scholarship: Literature, Theory, and the Environment*. Ed. Steven Rosendale. Iowa City: U of Iowa P, 2002. 42–58.

Fothergill, Robert A. "One Day at a Time: The Diary as Lifewriting." *Auto / Biography Studies* 10 (1995): 81–91.

Garrard, Greg. *Ecocriticism*. The New Critical Idiom. Oxford: Routledge, 2004.

Gill, Stephen, ed. *William Wordsworth*. The Oxford Authors. Oxford: Oxford UP, 1984.

———. *William Wordsworth: a Life*. New York: Oxford UP, 1989.

Gilligan, Carol. *In a Different Voice*. Cambridge: Harvard UP, 1982.

Gittings, Robert, and Jo Manton. *Dorothy Wordsworth*. Oxford: Oxford UP, 1985.

Glendening, John. *The High Road: Romantic Tourism, Scotland, and Literature, 1720–1820*. New York: St. Martin's, 1997.

Hill, Alan G., ed. *The Letters of Dorothy Wordsworth*. Oxford: Oxford UP, 1981.

Holmes, Richard. *Coleridge: Early Visions*. London: Harper Collins, 1998.

Homans, Margaret. *Bearing the Word: Language and Female Experience in Nineteenth-Century Women's Writing*. Chicago: U of Chicago P, 1986.

———. *Women Writers and Poetic Identity: Dorothy Wordsworth, Emily Bronte, and Emily Dickinson.* Princeton: Princeton UP, 1980.

Johnston, Kenneth R. *The Hidden Wordsworth: Poet, Lover, Rebel, Spy.* New York: Norton, 1998.

———. *Wordsworth and* The Recluse. New Haven: Yale UP, 1984.

Kelly, Gary. "Death and the Matron: Felicia Hemans, Romantic Death, and the Founding of the Modern Liberal State." *Felicia Hemans: Reimagining Poetry in the Nineteenth Century.* Ed. Nanora Sweet and Julie Melnyk. New York: Palgrave, 2001. 196–211.

Ketcham, Carl. "Dorothy Wordsworth's Journals, 1824–1835." *The Wordsworth Circle* 9 (1978): 3–16.

Kroeber, Karl. *Ecological Literary Criticism: Romantic Imagining and the Biology of Mind.* New York: Columbia UP, 1994.

———. "'Home at Grasmere': Ecological Holiness." *PMLA* 89 (1974): 32–41.

Levin, Susan. *Dorothy Wordsworth and Romanticism.* New Brunswick: Rutgers UP, 1987.

McCormick, Anita Hemphill. "'I shall be beloved—I want no more': Dorothy Wordsworth's Rhetoric and the Appeal to Feeling in *The Grasmere Journals.*" *Philological Quarterly* 69 (1990): 471–93.

McGavran, James Holt, Jr. "Dorothy Wordsworth's Journals: Putting Herself Down." *The Private Self: Theory and Practice of Women's Autobiographical Writings.* Ed. Shari Benstock. Chapel Hill: U of North Carolina P, 1988. 230–53.

McKusick, James C. *Green Writing: Romanticism and Ecology.* New York: St. Martin's, 2000.

Mellin, Robert. "Dorothy Wordsworth, Ecology, and the Picturesque." *Reading the Earth: New Directions in the Study of Literature and the Environment.* Ed. Michael P. Branch, et al. Moscow: U of Idaho P, 1998. 67–78.

Mellor, Anne K. *Romanticism and Gender.* New York: Routledge, 1993.

Merchant, Carolyn. *The Death of Nature: Women, Ecology, and the Scientific Revolution.* San Francisco: Harper and Row, 1980.

Miller, Jean Baker. *Toward a New Psychology of Women.* Boston: Beacon, 1976.

Nabholtz, John R. "Dorothy Wordsworth and the Picturesque." *Studies in Romanticism* 3 (1964). 118–28.

Oerlemans, Onno. *Romanticism and the Materiality of Nature.* Toronto: U of Toronto P, 2002.

Ortner, Sherry. "Is Female to Male as Nature is to Culture?" *Women, Culture, and Society.* Eds. Michelle Rosaldo and Louise Lamphere. Stanford: Stanford UP, 1974. 67–87.

Packard, William. *The Poet's Dictionary: A Handbook of Prosody and Poetic Devices.* New York: Harper Collins, 1989.

Rosendale, Steven, ed. *The Greening of Literary Scholarship: Literature, Theory, and the Environment.* Iowa City: U of Iowa P, 2002.

Ruskin, John. *The Literary Criticism of John Ruskin*. Ed. Harold Bloom. New York: De Capo, 1965.

Schor, Naomi. *Reading in Detail: Aesthetics and the Feminine*. New York: Methuen, 1987.

Simpson, David. *The Academic Postmodern and the Rule of Literature: A Report on Half-Knowledge*. Chicago: U of Chicago P, 1995.

Snyder, Gary. *Axe Handles*. San Francisco: North Point Press, 1983.

———. *The Real Work: Interviews and Talks 1964–1979*. San Francisco: New Directions, 1980.

Walker, Carol Kyros. Introduction. *Recollections of a Tour Made in Scotland*. By Dorothy Wordsworth. New Haven: Yale, 1997. 1–26.

Wolfson, Susan J. "Individual in Community: Dorothy Wordsworth in Conversation with William." *Romanticism and Feminism*. Ed. Anne K. Mellor. Bloomington: Indiana UP, 1988. 139–66.

Woof, Pamela. "Dorothy Wordsworth, *Journals*." *A Companion to Romanticism*. Ed. Duncan Wu. Oxford: Blackwell, 1999. 157–68.

———. *Dorothy Wordsworth, Writer*. Grasmere, Cumbria: The Wordsworth Trust, 1988.

Wordsworth, Dorothy. *A Narrative Concerning George and Sarah Green of the Parish of Grasmere, Addressed to a Friend*. Ed. E. de Selincourt. Oxford: Clarendon, 1936.

———. *Journals of Dorothy Wordsworth*. Ed. E. de Selincourt. Vol. I. London: MacMillan, 1952.

———. *The Grasmere and Alfoxden Journals*. Ed. Pamela Woof. Oxford: Oxford UP, 2002.

Wordsworth, Jonathan. "On Man, on Nature, and on Human Life." *RES* 31 (1980): 2–29.

Wordsworth, William. *Selected Prose*. Ed. John O. Hayden. London: Penguin, 1988.

———. *The Poetical Works of William Wordsworth*. Ed. Ernest de Selincourt and Helen Darbishire. Vol. 5. Oxford: Clarendon, 1949.

Wordsworth, William, and Dorothy Wordsworth. *The Letters of William and Dorothy Wordsworth: The Early Years, 1787–1805*. Ed. Alan G. Hill, Mary Moorman, and Chester L. Shaver. Oxford: Clarendon, 1967.

———. *The Letters of William and Dorothy Wordsworth: The Middle Years, Part I, 1806–1811*. Ed. E. de Selincourt. Rev. ed. Mary Moorman. Oxford: Clarendon, 1969.

———. *The Letters of William and Dorothy Wordsworth: The Middle Years, Part II, 1812–1820*. Ed. E. de Selincourt. Rev. ed. Mary Moorman and Alan G. Hill. Oxford: Clarendon, 1970.

Worster, Donald. *Nature's Economy: A History of Ecological Ideas*. Second Ed. Cambridge: Cambridge UP, 1994.

Worthen, John. *The Gang: Coleridge, the Hutchinsons & the Wordsworths in 1802*. New Haven: Yale UP, 2001.

Wu, Duncan, ed. *Romantic Women Poets: an Anthology*. Oxford: Blackwell, 1997.

Index